WILLIAM SHAKESPEARE

AS YOU LIKE IT

CLASSICS

Published 2024

FiNGERPRINT! CLASSiCS
Prakash Books

Fingerprint Publishing
@FingerprintP
@fingerprintpublishingbooks
www.fingerprintpublishing.com

ISBN: 978 93 8956 718 2

William Shakespeare began his career as an actor, writer, and part owner of a playing company called the Lord Chamberlain's Men, later known as King's Men, in London. Often regarded as the 'Bard of Avon' he is one of the world's pre-eminent dramatists. Born and brought up in Stratford-upon-Avon, he married Anne Hathaway at the age of eighteen and they had three children—Susanna, and twins Hamnet and Judith. Though few records survive of his private life, he appeared to have retired to Stratford around 1613 where he died three years later.

His works still in existence, including some collaborations, consist of thirty-eight plays, one hundred and fifty-four sonnets, two long narrative poems, and several other verses. His plays are performed much more than any other playwright's and have been translated in almost all major languages. Most of his known works have been produced between 1589 and 1613. His early plays were mainly comedies and histories which remain regarded as some of the best works produced in these genres.

Shakespeare's plays are difficult to date. His early classical and Italianate comedies contain tight double plots and precise comic sequences giving way to the romantic atmosphere of his most acclaimed comedies in the mid-1590s. *A Midsummer Night's Dream*—a witty mixture of romance, fairy magic, and comic low life scenes—is one of his most delightful creations shortly before he turned to *Romeo and Juliet*. *Romeo and Juliet* is his most famous romantic tragedy of sexually charged adolescence, love, and death. It marks a departure from his earlier works and from others of the English Renaissance.

His plays demonstrate the expansiveness of his imagination and the extent of his learning. Shakespeare's sequence of great comedies continues with *Merchant of Venice*, *Much Ado About Nothing*, *As You Like It*, and *Twelfth Night*. Featuring one of the most popular and charming heroines of Shakespeare, Rosalind, *As You Like It* is a drama of artifice, gender reversals, exile, and homoeroticism. Though some critics consider this a work of lesser quality as compared to his other plays, this remarkable pastoral comedy continues to remain as delightful as ever.

Shakespeare introduced prose comedy in the histories of the late 1590s—*Henry IV*, *Part I* and *Part II*, and *Henry V*—after the lyrical *Richard II*. *Julius Caesar* introduced a new kind of drama. Based on true events from Roman history, it is one of Shakespeare's most loved political tragedies.

Shakespeare wrote the so-called 'problem plays' in the early 17th century. *Measure for Measure, Troilus and Cressida*, and *All's Well that Ends Well* being a few of them. Until about 1608, he mainly wrote tragedies including *Hamlet, Othello, King Lear*, and *Macbeth*.

Antony and Cleopatra and *Coriolanus*—his last major tragedies, contain some of his finest poetry. Shakespeare wrote tragicomedies, also known as romances, in his last phase. These include *Cymbeline, The Winter's Tale*, and *The Tempest*, as well as the collaboration *Pericles, Prince of Tyre*.

A true genius, Shakespeare's popular characters and plots are studied, performed, reinterpreted, and discussed till today. William Shakespeare, known as the English national poet, is considered the greatest dramatist of all time.

CHARACTERS OF THE PLAY

DUKE, living in exile
FREDERICK, his Brother, Usurper of his Dominions
AMIENS } Lords attending upon the
JAQUES } banished Duke
LE BEAU, a Courtier, attending upon Frederick
CHARLES, a Wrestler to Frederick
OLIVER
JAQUES } Sons of Sir Rowland de Boys
ORLANDO
ADAM
DENNIS } Servants to Oliver
TOUCHSTONE, the court jester
SIR OLIVER MARTEXT, a Vicar
CORIN
SILVIUS } Shepherds

WILLIAM, a Country Fellow, in love with Audrey
A person representing Hymen
ROSALIND, Daughter to the banished Duke
CELIA, Daughter to Frederick
PHEBE, a Shepherdess
AUDREY, a Country Wench
Lords, Pages, Foresters, and Attendants

SCENE:
OLIVER'S ORCHARD
NEAR HIS HOUSE;
THE USURPER'S COURT;
AND THE FOREST OF ARDEN

Act 1

SCENE I.
ORCHARD OF OLIVER'S HOUSE.

Enter ORLANDO and ADAM

ORLANDO

As I remember, Adam, it was upon this fashion bequeathed me by will but poor a thousand crowns, and, as thou sayest, charged my brother, on his blessing, to breed me well; and there begins my sadness. My brother Jaques he keeps at school, and report speaks goldenly of his profit. For my part, he keeps me rustically at home, or, to speak more properly, stays me here at home unkept; for call you that keeping for a gentleman of my birth, that differs not from the stalling of an ox? His horses are bred better; for, besides that they are fair with their feeding, they are taught their manage, and to that end riders dearly hired; but I, his brother, gain nothing under him but growth; for the which his animals on his dunghills are as much bound to him as I. Besides this nothing that he so plentifully gives me, the something that nature gave me his countenance seems to take from me. He lets me feed with his hinds, bars me the place of a brother, and, as much as in him lies, mines my gentility with my education. This is it, Adam, that grieves me; and the spirit of my father, which I think is within me, begins to mutiny against this servitude. I will no longer endure it, though yet I know no wise remedy how to avoid it.

Enter OLIVER

ADAM

Yonder comes my master, your brother.

ORLANDO

Go apart, Adam, and thou shalt hear how he will shake me up. [*ADAM retires*]

OLIVER

Now, sir! what make you here?

ORLANDO

Nothing; I am not taught to make any thing.

OLIVER

What mar you then, sir?

ORLANDO

Marry, sir, I am helping you to mar that which God made, a poor unworthy brother of yours, with idleness.

OLIVER

Marry, sir, be better employed, and be naught awhile.

ORLANDO

Shall I keep your hogs and eat husks with them? What prodigal portion have I spent, that I should come to such penury?

OLIVER

Know you where your are, sir?

ORLANDO

O, sir, very well; here in your orchard.

OLIVER

Know you before whom, sir?

ORLANDO

Ay, better than him I am before knows me. I know you are my eldest brother; and, in the gentle condition of blood, you should so know me. The courtesy of nations allows you my better, in that you are the first-born; but the same tradition takes not away my blood, were there twenty brothers betwixt us. I have as much of my father in me as you; albeit, I confess, your coming before me is nearer to his reverence.

OLIVER

What, boy! [*Strikes him*]

ORLANDO

Come, come, elder brother, you are too young in this.

OLIVER

Wilt thou lay hands on me, villain?

ORLANDO

I am no villain; I am the youngest son of Sir Rowland de Boys; he was my father, and he is thrice a villain that says such a father begot villains. Wert thou not my brother, I would not take this hand from thy throat till this other had pulled out thy tongue for saying so. Thou hast railed on thyself.

ADAM

Sweet masters, be patient; for your father's remembrance, be at accord.

OLIVER

Let me go, I say.

ORLANDO

I will not, till I please; you shall hear me. My father charged you in his will to give me good education: you have trained me like a peasant, obscuring and hiding from me all gentleman-like qualities. The spirit of my father grows strong in me, and I will no longer endure it;

therefore allow me such exercises as may become a gentleman, or give me the poor allottery my father left me by testament; with that I will go buy my fortunes.

OLIVER

And what wilt thou do? Beg, when that is spent? Well, sir, get you in. I will not long be troubled with you; you shall have some part of your will. I pray you, leave me.

ORLANDO

I will no further offend you than becomes me for my good.

OLIVER

Get you with him, you old dog.

ADAM

Is 'old dog' my reward? Most true, I have lost my teeth in your service. God be with my old master! He would not have spoke such a word.

Exeunt ORLANDO and
ADAM

OLIVER

Is it even so? Begin you to grow upon me? I will physic your rankness, and yet give no thousand crowns neither. Holla, Dennis!

Enter DENNIS

DENNIS

Calls your worship?

OLIVER

Was not Charles, the Duke's wrestler, here to speak with me?

DENNIS

So please you, he is here at the door and importunes access to you.

OLIVER

Call him in.

Exit DENNIS

'Twill be a good way; and to-morrow the wrestling is.

Enter CHARLES

CHARLES

Good morrow to your worship.

OLIVER

Good Monsieur Charles, what's the new news at the new court?

CHARLES

There's no news at the court, sir, but the old news; that is, the old Duke is banished by his younger brother the new Duke; and three or four loving lords have put themselves into voluntary exile with him, whose lands and revenues enrich the new Duke; therefore he gives them good leave to wander.

OLIVER

Can you tell if Rosalind, the Duke's daughter, be banished with her father?

CHARLES

O, no; for the Duke's daughter, her cousin, so loves her, being ever from their cradles bred together, that she would have followed her exile, or have died to stay behind her. She is at the court, and no less beloved of her uncle than his own daughter; and never two ladies loved as they do.

OLIVER

Where will the old Duke live?

CHARLES

They say he is already in the Forest of Arden, and a many merry men with him; and there they live like the old Robin Hood of England. They say many young gentlemen flock to him every day, and fleet the time carelessly, as they did in the golden world.

OLIVER

What, you wrestle to-morrow before the new Duke?

CHARLES

Marry, do I, sir; and I came to acquaint you with a matter. I am given, sir, secretly to understand that your younger brother Orlando hath a disposition to come in disguised against me to try a fall. To-morrow, sir, I wrestle for my credit; and he that escapes me without some broken limb shall acquit him well. Your brother is but young and tender; and, for your love, I would be loath to foil him, as I must, for my own honour, if he come in; therefore, out of my love to you, I came hither to acquaint you withal, that either you might stay him from his intendment or brook such disgrace well as he shall run into, in that it is a thing of his own search and altogether against my will.

OLIVER

Charles, I thank thee for thy love to me, which thou shalt find I will most kindly requite. I had myself notice of my brother's purpose herein and have by underhand means laboured to dissuade him from it, but he is resolute. I'll tell thee, Charles, it is the stubbornest young fellow of France, full of ambition, an envious emulator of every man's good parts, a secret and villainous contriver against me his natural brother. Therefore use thy discretion: I had as lief thou didst break his neck as his finger. And thou wert best look to't; for if thou dost him any slight disgrace or if he do not mightily grace himself on thee, he will practise against thee by poison, entrap thee by some treacherous device and never leave thee till he hath ta'en thy life by some indirect means or other; for, I assure thee, and almost with tears I speak it, there is not one so young and so villainous this day living. I speak but brotherly of him; but should I anatomize him to thee as he is, I must blush and weep and thou must look pale and wonder.

CHARLES

I am heartily glad I came hither to you. If he come to-morrow, I'll give him his payment. If ever he go alone again, I'll never wrestle for prize more. And so God keep your worship!

OLIVER

Farewell, good Charles.

Exit CHARLES

Now will I stir this gamester. I hope I shall see an end of him; for my soul, yet I know not why, hates nothing more than he. Yet he's gentle, never schooled and yet learned, full of noble device, of all sorts enchantingly beloved, and indeed so much in the heart of the world, and especially of my own people, who best know him, that I am altogether misprised. But it shall not be so long; this wrestler shall clear

all. Nothing remains but that I kindle the boy
thither; which now I'll go about.

Exit

SCENE II. LAWN BEFORE
THE DUKE'S PALACE.

Enter CELIA and ROSALIND

CELIA

I pray thee, Rosalind, sweet my coz, be merry.

ROSALIND

Dear Celia, I show more mirth than I am
mistress of; and would you yet I were merrier?
Unless you could teach me to forget a banished
father, you must not learn me how to remember
any extraordinary pleasure.

CELIA

Herein I see thou lovest me not with the full
weight that I love thee. If my uncle, thy banished
father, had banished thy uncle, the Duke my
father, so thou hadst been still with me, I could
have taught my love to take thy father for mine;
so wouldst thou, if the truth of thy love to me
were so righteously tempered as mine is to thee.

ROSALIND

Well, I will forget the condition of my estate, to
rejoice in yours.

CELIA

> You know my father hath no child but I, nor none is like to have; and, truly, when he dies, thou shalt be his heir, for what he hath taken away from thy father perforce, I will render thee again in affection; by mine honour, I will; and when I break that oath, let me turn monster; therefore, my sweet Rose, my dear Rose, be merry.

ROSALIND

> From henceforth I will, coz, and devise sports. Let me see; what think you of falling in love?

CELIA

> Marry, I prithee, do, to make sport withal; but love no man in good earnest; nor no further in sport neither than with safety of a pure blush thou mayst in honour come off again.

ROSALIND

> What shall be our sport, then?

CELIA

> Let us sit and mock the good housewife Fortune from her wheel, that her gifts may henceforth be bestowed equally.

ROSALIND

> I would we could do so, for her benefits are mightily misplaced, and the bountiful blind woman doth most mistake in her gifts to women.

CELIA

'Tis true; for those that she makes fair she scarce makes honest, and those that she makes honest she makes very ill-favouredly.

ROSALIND

Nay, now thou goest from Fortune's office to Nature's: Fortune reigns in gifts of the world, not in the lineaments of Nature.

Enter TOUCHSTONE

CELIA

No? When Nature hath made a fair creature, may she not by Fortune fall into the fire? Though Nature hath given us wit to flout at Fortune, hath not Fortune sent in this fool to cut off the argument?

ROSALIND

Indeed, there is Fortune too hard for Nature, when Fortune makes Nature's natural the cutter-off of Nature's wit.

CELIA

Peradventure this is not Fortune's work neither, but Nature's; who perceiveth our natural wits too dull to reason of such goddesses and hath sent this natural for our whetstone; for always the dullness of the fool is the whetstone of the wits. How now, wit! Whither wander you?

TOUCHSTONE

Mistress, you must come away to your father.

CELIA

Were you made the messenger?

TOUCHSTONE

No, by mine honour, but I was bid to come for you.

ROSALIND

Where learned you that oath, fool?

TOUCHSTONE

Of a certain knight that swore by his honour they were good pancakes and swore by his honour the mustard was naught. Now I'll stand to it, the pancakes were naught and the mustard was good, and yet was not the knight forsworn.

CELIA

How prove you that, in the great heap of your knowledge?

ROSALIND

Ay, marry, now unmuzzle your wisdom.

TOUCHSTONE

Stand you both forth now: stroke your chins, and swear by your beards that I am a knave.

CELIA

By our beards, if we had them, thou art.

TOUCHSTONE

By my knavery, if I had it, then I were; but if you swear by that that is not, you are not forsworn; no more was this knight swearing by his honour, for he never had any; or if he had, he had sworn it away before ever he saw those pancakes or that mustard.

CELIA

Prithee, who is't that thou meanest?

TOUCHSTONE

One that old Frederick, your father, loves.

CELIA

My father's love is enough to honour him. Enough! Speak no more of him; you'll be whipped for taxation one of these days.

TOUCHSTONE

The more pity, that fools may not speak wisely what wise men do foolishly.

CELIA

By my troth, thou sayest true; for since the little wit that fools have was silenced, the little foolery that wise men have makes a great show. Here comes Monsieur Le Beau.

ROSALIND

With his mouth full of news.

CELIA

Which he will put on us, as pigeons feed their young.

ROSALIND

Then shall we be news-crammed.

CELIA

All the better; we shall be the more marketable.

Enter LE BEAU

Bon jour, Monsieur Le Beau. What's the news?

LE BEAU

Fair princess, you have lost much good sport.

CELIA

Sport! of what colour?

LE BEAU

What colour, madam? How shall I answer you?

ROSALIND

As wit and fortune will.

TOUCHSTONE

Or as the Destinies decree.

CELIA

Well said; that was laid on with a trowel.

TOUCHSTONE

Nay, if I keep not my rank—

ROSALIND

Thou losest thy old smell.

LE BEAU

You amaze me, ladies. I would have told you of good wrestling, which you have lost the sight of.

ROSALIND

You tell us the manner of the wrestling.

LE BEAU

I will tell you the beginning; and, if it please your ladyships, you may see the end; for the best is yet to do; and here, where you are, they are coming to perform it.

CELIA

Well, the beginning, that is dead and buried.

LE BEAU

There comes an old man and his three sons—

CELIA

I could match this beginning with an old tale.

LE BEAU

Three proper young men, of excellent growth and presence.

ROSALIND

With bills on their necks, 'Be it known unto all men by these presents.'

LE BEAU

The eldest of the three wrestled with Charles, the Duke's wrestler; which Charles in a moment threw him and broke three of his ribs, that there is little hope of life in him. So he served the second, and so the third. Yonder they lie; the poor old man, their father, making such pitiful dole over them that all the beholders take his part with weeping.

ROSALIND

Alas!

TOUCHSTONE

But what is the sport, monsieur, that the ladies have lost?

LE BEAU

Why, this that I speak of.

TOUCHSTONE

Thus men may grow wiser every day. It is the first time that ever I heard breaking of ribs was sport for ladies.

CELIA

Or I, I promise thee.

ROSALIND

But is there any else longs to see this broken music in his sides? Is there yet another dotes upon rib-breaking? Shall we see this wrestling, cousin?

LE BEAU

You must, if you stay here; for here is the place appointed for the wrestling, and they are ready to perform it.

CELIA

Yonder, sure, they are coming. Let us now stay and see it.

Flourish. Enter DUKE FREDERICK,
Lords, ORLANDO,
CHARLES, and Attendants

DUKE FREDERICK

Come on; since the youth will not be entreated, his own peril on his forwardness.

ROSALIND

Is yonder the man?

LE BEAU

Even he, madam.

CELIA

Alas, he is too young! yet he looks successfully.

DUKE FREDERICK

How now, daughter and cousin! Are you crept hither to see the wrestling?

ROSALIND

Ay, my liege, so please you give us leave.

DUKE FREDERICK

You will take little delight in it, I can tell you; there is such odds in the man. In pity of the challenger's youth I would fain dissuade him, but he will not be entreated. Speak to him, ladies; see if you can move him.

CELIA

Call him hither, good Monsieur Le Beau.

DUKE FREDERICK

Do so; I'll not be by.

DUKE FREDERICK goes apart

LE BEAU

Monsieur the challenger, the princesses call for you.

ORLANDO

I attend them with all respect and duty.

ROSALIND

Young man, have you challenged Charles the wrestler?

ORLANDO

No, fair princess; he is the general challenger. I come but in, as others do, to try with him the strength of my youth.

CELIA

Young gentleman, your spirits are too bold for your years. You have seen cruel proof of this man's strength; if you saw yourself with your eyes or knew yourself with your judgment, the fear of your adventure would counsel you to a more equal enterprise. We pray you, for your own sake, to embrace your own safety and give over this attempt.

ROSALIND

Do, young sir; your reputation shall not therefore be misprised: we will make it our suit to the Duke that the wrestling might not go forward.

ORLANDO

I beseech you, punish me not with your hard thoughts; wherein I confess me much guilty, to deny so fair and excellent ladies any thing. But let your fair eyes and gentle wishes go with me to my trial; wherein if I be foiled, there is but one shamed that was never gracious; if killed, but one dead that is willing to be so. I shall do my friends no wrong, for I have none to lament me, the world no injury, for in it I have nothing; only in the world I fill up a place, which may be better supplied when I have made it empty.

ROSALIND

The little strength that I have, I would it were with you.

CELIA

And mine, to eke out hers.

ROSALIND

Fare you well. Pray heaven I be deceived in you!

CELIA

Your heart's desires be with you!

CHARLES

Come, where is this young gallant that is so desirous to lie with his mother earth?

ORLANDO

Ready, sir; but his will hath in it a more modest working.

DUKE FREDERICK

You shall try but one fall.

CHARLES

No, I warrant your grace, you shall not entreat him to a second, that have so mightily persuaded him from a first.

ORLANDO

An you mean to mock me after, you should not have mocked me before; but come your ways.

ROSALIND

Now Hercules be thy speed, young man!

CELIA

I would I were invisible, to catch the strong fellow by the leg. [*They wrestle*]

ROSALIND

O excellent young man!

CELIA

If I had a thunderbolt in mine eye, I can tell who should down.

> *Shout. CHARLES is thrown*

DUKE FREDERICK

No more, no more.

ORLANDO

Yes, I beseech your grace; I am not yet well breathed.

DUKE FREDERICK

How dost thou, Charles?

LE BEAU

He cannot speak, my lord.

DUKE FREDERICK

Bear him away. What is thy name, young man?

ORLANDO

Orlando, my liege; the youngest son of Sir Rowland de Boys.

DUKE FREDERICK

I would thou hadst been son to some man else.
The world esteem'd thy father honourable,
But I did find him still mine enemy.
Thou shouldst have better pleased me with this
 deed,
Hadst thou descended from another house.
But fare thee well; thou art a gallant youth;
I would thou hadst told me of another father.

*Exeunt DUKE FREDERICK,
train, and LE BEAU*

CELIA

Were I my father, coz, would I do this?

ORLANDO

> I am more proud to be Sir Rowland's son,
> His youngest son; and would not change that
>> calling,
> To be adopted heir to Frederick.

ROSALIND

> My father loved Sir Rowland as his soul,
> And all the world was of my father's mind;
> Had I before known this young man his son,
> I should have given him tears unto entreaties,
> Ere he should thus have ventured.

CELIA

> Gentle cousin,
> Let us go thank him and encourage him;
> My father's rough and envious disposition
> Sticks me at heart. Sir, you have well deserved;
> If you do keep your promises in love
> But justly, as you have exceeded all promise,
> Your mistress shall be happy.

ROSALIND

> Gentleman,
> *Giving him a chain from her neck*
> Wear this for me, one out of suits with fortune,
> That could give more, but that her hand lacks
>> means.
> Shall we go, coz?

CELIA

Ay. Fare you well, fair gentleman.

ORLANDO

Can I not say, I thank you? My better parts

Are all thrown down, and that which here
stands up

Is but a quintain, a mere lifeless block.

ROSALIND

He calls us back. My pride fell with my fortunes;

I'll ask him what he would. Did you call, sir?

Sir, you have wrestled well and overthrown

More than your enemies.

CELIA

Will you go, coz?

ROSALIND

Have with you. Fare you well.

Exeunt ROSALIND and
CELIA

ORLANDO

What passion hangs these weights upon my
tongue?

I cannot speak to her, yet she urged conference.

O poor Orlando, thou art overthrown!

Or Charles or something weaker masters thee.

Re-enter LE BEAU

LE BEAU

Good sir, I do in friendship counsel you

To leave this place. Albeit you have deserved
High commendation, true applause and love,
Yet such is now the Duke's condition
That he misconstrues all that you have done.
The Duke is humorous; what he is indeed,
More suits you to conceive than I to speak of.

ORLANDO

I thank you, sir; and, pray you, tell me this:
Which of the two was daughter of the Duke
That here was at the wrestling?

LE BEAU

Neither his daughter, if we judge by manners;
But yet indeed the lesser is his daughter
The other is daughter to the banish'd Duke,
And here detain'd by her usurping uncle,
To keep his daughter company; whose loves
Are dearer than the natural bond of sisters.
But I can tell you that of late this Duke
Hath ta'en displeasure 'gainst his gentle niece,
Grounded upon no other argument
But that the people praise her for her virtues
And pity her for her good father's sake;
And, on my life, his malice 'gainst the lady
Will suddenly break forth. Sir, fare you well.
Hereafter, in a better world than this,
I shall desire more love and knowledge of you.

ORLANDO

I rest much bounden to you; fare you well.

Exit LE BEAU

Thus must I from the smoke into the smother;
From tyrant Duke unto a tyrant brother.
But heavenly Rosalind!

Exit

SCENE III. A ROOM IN THE PALACE.

Enter CELIA and ROSALIND

CELIA

Why, cousin! why, Rosalind! Cupid have mercy!
Not a word?

ROSALIND

Not one to throw at a dog.

CELIA

No, thy words are too precious to be cast away
upon curs; throw some of them at me; come,
lame me with reasons.

ROSALIND

Then there were two cousins laid up; when
the one should be lamed with reasons and the
other mad without any.

CELIA

But is all this for your father?

ROSALIND

No, some of it is for my child's father. O, how
full of briers is this working-day world!

CELIA

They are but burs, cousin, thrown upon thee in
holiday foolery; if we walk not in the trodden
paths our very petticoats will catch them.

ROSALIND

I could shake them off my coat: these burs are
in my heart.

CELIA

Hem them away.

ROSALIND

I would try, if I could cry 'hem' and have him.

CELIA

Come, come, wrestle with thy affections.

ROSALIND

O, they take the part of a better wrestler than
myself!

CELIA

O, a good wish upon you! you will try in time,
in despite of a fall. But, turning these jests
out of service, let us talk in good earnest. Is
it possible, on such a sudden, you should fall
into so strong a liking with old Sir Rowland's
youngest son?

ROSALIND

The Duke my father loved his father dearly.

CELIA

Doth it therefore ensue that you should love his son dearly? By this kind of chase, I should hate him, for my father hated his father dearly; yet I hate not Orlando.

ROSALIND

No, faith, hate him not, for my sake.

CELIA

Why should I not? Doth he not deserve well?

ROSALIND

Let me love him for that, and do you love him because I do. Look, here comes the Duke.

CELIA

With his eyes full of anger.

Enter DUKE FREDERICK, with Lords

DUKE FREDERICK

Mistress, dispatch you with your safest haste
And get you from our court.

ROSALIND

Me, uncle?

DUKE FREDERICK

You, cousin
Within these ten days if that thou be'st found
So near our public court as twenty miles,
Thou diest for it.

ROSALIND

    I do beseech your grace,

    Let me the knowledge of my fault bear with me.

    If with myself I hold intelligence

    Or have acquaintance with mine own desires,

    If that I do not dream or be not frantic—

    As I do trust I am not—then, dear uncle,

    Never so much as in a thought unborn

    Did I offend your highness.

DUKE FREDERICK

    Thus do all traitors;

    If their purgation did consist in words,

    They are as innocent as grace itself.

    Let it suffice thee that I trust thee not.

ROSALIND

    Yet your mistrust cannot make me a traitor.

    Tell me whereon the likelihood depends.

DUKE FREDERICK

    Thou art thy father's daughter; there's enough.

ROSALIND

    So was I when your highness took his dukedom;

    So was I when your highness banish'd him.

    Treason is not inherited, my lord;

    Or, if we did derive it from our friends,

    What's that to me? My father was no traitor.

    Then, good my liege, mistake me not so much

    To think my poverty is treacherous.

CELIA

Dear sovereign, hear me speak.

DUKE FREDERICK

Ay, Celia; we stay'd her for your sake,
Else had she with her father ranged along.

CELIA

I did not then entreat to have her stay;
It was your pleasure and your own remorse;
I was too young that time to value her;
But now I know her. If she be a traitor,
Why so am I; we still have slept together,
Rose at an instant, learn'd, play'd, eat together,
And wheresoever we went, like Juno's swans,
Still we went coupled and inseparable.

DUKE FREDERICK

She is too subtle for thee; and her smoothness,
Her very silence and her patience
Speak to the people, and they pity her.
Thou art a fool. She robs thee of thy name;
And thou wilt show more bright and seem
    more virtuous
When she is gone. Then open not thy lips.
Firm and irrevocable is my doom
Which I have pass'd upon her; she is banish'd.

CELIA

Pronounce that sentence then on me, my liege;
I cannot live out of her company.

DUKE FREDERICK

> You are a fool. You, niece, provide yourself.
> If you outstay the time, upon mine honour,
> And in the greatness of my word, you die.
> > *Exeunt DUKE FREDERICK and Lords*

CELIA

> O my poor Rosalind, whither wilt thou go?
> Wilt thou change fathers? I will give thee mine.
> I charge thee, be not thou more grieved than
> > I am.

ROSALIND

> I have more cause.

CELIA

> Thou hast not, cousin;
> Prithee be cheerful. Know'st thou not, the
> > Duke
> Hath banish'd me, his daughter?

ROSALIND

> That he hath not.

CELIA

> No, hath not? Rosalind lacks then the love
> Which teacheth thee that thou and I am one.
> Shall we be sunder'd? Shall we part, sweet girl?
> No; let my father seek another heir.
> Therefore devise with me how we may fly,
> Whither to go and what to bear with us;
> And do not seek to take your change upon you,

To bear your griefs yourself and leave me out;
For, by this heaven, now at our sorrows pale,
Say what thou canst, I'll go along with thee.

ROSALIND

Why, whither shall we go?

CELIA

To seek my uncle in the Forest of Arden.

ROSALIND

Alas, what danger will it be to us,
Maids as we are, to travel forth so far!
Beauty provoketh thieves sooner than gold.

CELIA

I'll put myself in poor and mean attire
And with a kind of umber smirch my face;
The like do you; so shall we pass along
And never stir assailants.

ROSALIND

Were it not better,
Because that I am more than common tall,
That I did suit me all points like a man?
A gallant curtle-axe upon my thigh,
A boar-spear in my hand; and—in my heart
Lie there what hidden woman's fear there will—
We'll have a swashing and a martial outside,
As many other mannish cowards have
That do outface it with their semblances.

CELIA

What shall I call thee when thou art a man?

ROSALIND

I'll have no worse a name than Jove's own page;
And therefore look you call me Ganymede.
But what will you be call'd?

CELIA

Something that hath a reference to my state
No longer Celia, but Aliena.

ROSALIND

But, cousin, what if we assay'd to steal
The clownish fool out of your father's court?
Would he not be a comfort to our travel?

CELIA

He'll go along o'er the wide world with me;
Leave me alone to woo him. Let's away,
And get our jewels and our wealth together,
Devise the fittest time and safest way
To hide us from pursuit that will be made
After my flight. Now go we in content
To liberty and not to banishment.

Exeunt

Act 2

SCENE I. THE FOREST OF ARDEN.

Enter DUKE SENIOR, AMIENS, and two or three Lords, like foresters

DUKE SENIOR

    Now, my co-mates and brothers in exile,
    Hath not old custom made this life more sweet
    Than that of painted pomp? Are not these woods
    More free from peril than the envious court?
    Here feel we but the penalty of Adam,
    The seasons' difference, as the icy fang
    And churlish chiding of the winter's wind,
    Which, when it bites and blows upon my body,
    Even till I shrink with cold, I smile and say
    'This is no flattery; these are counsellors
    That feelingly persuade me what I am.'

Sweet are the uses of adversity,
Which, like the toad, ugly and venomous,
Wears yet a precious jewel in his head;
And this our life exempt from public haunt
Finds tongues in trees, books in the running
    brooks,
Sermons in stones and good in every thing.
I would not change it.

AMIENS

Happy is your grace,
That can translate the stubbornness of fortune
Into so quiet and so sweet a style.

DUKE SENIOR

Come, shall we go and kill us venison?
And yet it irks me the poor dappled fools,
Being native burghers of this desert city,
Should in their own confines with forked heads
Have their round haunches gored.

FIRST LORD

Indeed, my lord,
The melancholy Jaques grieves at that,
And, in that kind, swears you do more usurp
Than doth your brother that hath banish'd you.
To-day my Lord of Amiens and myself
Did steal behind him as he lay along
Under an oak whose antique root peeps out

Upon the brook that brawls along this wood!
To the which place a poor sequester'd stag,
That from the hunter's aim had ta'en a hurt,
Did come to languish, and indeed, my lord,
The wretched animal heaved forth such groans
That their discharge did stretch his leathern
     coat
Almost to bursting, and the big round tears
Coursed one another down his innocent nose
In piteous chase; and thus the hairy fool
Much marked of the melancholy Jaques,
Stood on the extremest verge of the swift
     brook,
Augmenting it with tears.

DUKE SENIOR

But what said Jaques?
Did he not moralize this spectacle?

FIRST LORD

O, yes, into a thousand similes.
First, for his weeping into the needless stream;
'Poor deer,' quoth he, 'thou makest a testament
As worldlings do, giving thy sum of more
To that which had too much.' Then, being there
     alone,
Left and abandon'd of his velvet friends,
''Tis right'; quoth he; 'thus misery doth part

The flux of company.' Anon a careless herd,
Full of the pasture, jumps along by him
And never stays to greet him; 'Ay' quoth Jaques,
'Sweep on, you fat and greasy citizens;
'Tis just the fashion. Wherefore do you look
Upon that poor and broken bankrupt there?'
Thus most invectively he pierceth through
The body of the country, city, court,
Yea, and of this our life, swearing that we
Are mere usurpers, tyrants and what's worse,
To fright the animals and to kill them up
In their assign'd and native dwelling-place.

DUKE SENIOR

And did you leave him in this contemplation?

SECOND LORD

We did, my lord, weeping and commenting
Upon the sobbing deer.

DUKE SENIOR

Show me the place;
I love to cope him in these sullen fits,
For then he's full of matter.

FIRST LORD

I'll bring you to him straight.

Exeunt

SCENE II. A ROOM IN THE PALACE.

Enter DUKE FREDERICK, with Lords

DUKE FREDERICK

    Can it be possible that no man saw them?

    It cannot be; some villains of my court

    Are of consent and sufferance in this.

FIRST LORD

    I cannot hear of any that did see her.

    The ladies, her attendants of her chamber,

    Saw her abed, and in the morning early

    They found the bed untreasured of their mistress.

SECOND LORD

    My lord, the roynish clown, at whom so oft

    Your grace was wont to laugh, is also missing.

    Hisperia, the princess' gentlewoman,

    Confesses that she secretly o'erheard

    Your daughter and her cousin much commend

    The parts and graces of the wrestler

    That did but lately foil the sinewy Charles;

    And she believes, wherever they are gone,

    That youth is surely in their company.

DUKE FREDERICK

    Send to his brother; fetch that gallant hither;

    If he be absent, bring his brother to me;

    I'll make him find him. Do this suddenly,

And let not search and inquisition quail
To bring again these foolish runaways.

Exeunt

SCENE III. BEFORE OLIVER'S HOUSE.

Enter ORLANDO and ADAM, meeting
ORLANDO
    Who's there?
ADAM
    What, my young master? O, my gentle master!
    O my sweet master! O you memory
    Of old Sir Rowland! why, what make you here?
    Why are you virtuous? Why do people love
        you?
    And wherefore are you gentle, strong and
        valiant?
    Why would you be so fond to overcome
    The bonny prizer of the humorous Duke?
    Your praise is come too swiftly home before
        you.
    Know you not, master, to some kind of men
    Their graces serve them but as enemies?
    No more do yours. Your virtues, gentle master,
    Are sanctified and holy traitors to you.
    O, what a world is this, when what is comely
    Envenoms him that bears it!

ORLANDO

Why, what's the matter?

ADAM

O unhappy youth!

Come not within these doors; within this roof

The enemy of all your graces lives.

Your brother—no, no brother; yet the son—

Yet not the son, I will not call him son

Of him I was about to call his father—

Hath heard your praises, and this night he means

To burn the lodging where you use to lie

And you within it. If he fail of that,

He will have other means to cut you off.

I overheard him and his practises.

This is no place; this house is but a butchery;

Abhor it, fear it, do not enter it.

ORLANDO

Why, whither, Adam, wouldst thou have me go?

ADAM

No matter whither, so you come not here.

ORLANDO

What, wouldst thou have me go and beg my food?

Or with a base and boisterous sword enforce

A thievish living on the common road?

This I must do, or know not what to do;
Yet this I will not do, do how I can.
I rather will subject me to the malice
Of a diverted blood and bloody brother.

ADAM

But do not so. I have five hundred crowns,
The thrifty hire I saved under your father,
Which I did store to be my foster-nurse
When service should in my old limbs lie lame
And unregarded age in corners thrown.
Take that, and He that doth the ravens feed,
Yea, providently caters for the sparrow,
Be comfort to my age! Here is the gold;
And all this I give you. Let me be your servant;
Though I look old, yet I am strong and lusty;
For in my youth I never did apply
Hot and rebellious liquors in my blood,
Nor did not with unbashful forehead woo
The means of weakness and debility;
Therefore my age is as a lusty winter,
Frosty, but kindly. Let me go with you;
I'll do the service of a younger man
In all your business and necessities.

ORLANDO

O good old man, how well in thee appears
The constant service of the antique world,
When service sweat for duty, not for meed!

Thou art not for the fashion of these times,
Where none will sweat but for promotion,
And having that, do choke their service up
Even with the having; it is not so with thee.
But, poor old man, thou prunest a rotten tree,
That cannot so much as a blossom yield
In lieu of all thy pains and husbandry
But come thy ways; well go along together,
And ere we have thy youthful wages spent,
We'll light upon some settled low content.

ADAM

Master, go on, and I will follow thee,
To the last gasp, with truth and loyalty.
From seventeen years till now almost fourscore
Here lived I, but now live here no more.
At seventeen years many their fortunes seek;
But at fourscore it is too late a week;
Yet fortune cannot recompense me better
Than to die well and not my master's debtor.

Exeunt

SCENE IV. THE FOREST OF ARDEN.

Enter ROSALIND for GANYMEDE, CELIA for ALIENA, and TOUCHSTONE

ROSALIND

O Jupiter, how weary are my spirits!

TOUCHSTONE

I care not for my spirits, if my legs were not weary.

ROSALIND

I could find in my heart to disgrace my man's apparel and to cry like a woman; but I must comfort the weaker vessel, as doublet and hose ought to show itself courageous to petticoat; therefore courage, good Aliena!

CELIA

I pray you, bear with me; I cannot go no further.

TOUCHSTONE

For my part, I had rather bear with you than bear you; yet I should bear no cross if I did bear you, for I think you have no money in your purse.

ROSALIND

Well, this is the Forest of Arden.

TOUCHSTONE

Ay, now am I in Arden; the more fool I; when I was at home, I was in a better place; but travellers must be content.

ROSALIND

Ay, be so, good Touchstone.

Enter CORIN and SILVIUS

Look you, who comes here; a young man and an old in solemn talk.

CORIN

    That is the way to make her scorn you still.

SILVIUS

    O Corin, that thou knew'st how I do love her!

CORIN

    I partly guess; for I have loved ere now.

SILVIUS

    No, Corin, being old, thou canst not guess,

    Though in thy youth thou wast as true a lover

    As ever sigh'd upon a midnight pillow.

    But if thy love were ever like to mine—

    As sure I think did never man love so—

    How many actions most ridiculous

    Hast thou been drawn to by thy fantasy?

CORIN

    Into a thousand that I have forgotten.

SILVIUS

    O, thou didst then ne'er love so heartily!

    If thou remember'st not the slightest folly

    That ever love did make thee run into,

    Thou hast not loved;

    Or if thou hast not sat as I do now,

    Wearying thy hearer in thy mistress' praise,

    Thou hast not loved;

    Or if thou hast not broke from company

    Abruptly, as my passion now makes me,

    Thou hast not loved.

O Phebe, Phebe, Phebe!

Exit SILVIUS

ROSALIND

Alas, poor shepherd! searching of thy wound,
I have by hard adventure found mine own.

TOUCHSTONE

And I mine. I remember, when I was in love
I broke my sword upon a stone and bid him
take that for coming a-night to Jane Smile;
and I remember the kissing of her batlet and
the cow's dugs that her pretty chopt hands
had milked; and I remember the wooing of
a peascod instead of her, from whom I took
two cods and, giving her them again, said with
weeping tears 'Wear these for my sake.' We
that are true lovers run into strange capers; but
as all is mortal in nature, so is all nature in love
mortal in folly.

ROSALIND

Thou speakest wiser than thou art ware of.

TOUCHSTONE

Nay, I shall ne'er be ware of mine own wit till I
break my shins against it.

ROSALIND

Jove, Jove! this shepherd's passion
Is much upon my fashion.

TOUCHSTONE

And mine; but it grows something stale with
me.

CELIA

I pray you, one of you question yond man
If he for gold will give us any food;
I faint almost to death.

TOUCHSTONE

Holla, you clown!

ROSALIND

Peace, fool; he's not thy kinsman.

CORIN

Who calls?

TOUCHSTONE

Your betters, sir.

CORIN

Else are they very wretched.

ROSALIND

Peace, I say. Good even to you, friend.

CORIN

And to you, gentle sir, and to you all.

ROSALIND

I prithee, shepherd, if that love or gold
Can in this desert place buy entertainment,
Bring us where we may rest ourselves and feed.
Here's a young maid with travel much oppress'd
And faints for succor.

CORIN

    Fair sir, I pity her

    And wish, for her sake more than for mine
        own,

    My fortunes were more able to relieve her;

    But I am shepherd to another man

    And do not shear the fleeces that I graze.

    My master is of churlish disposition

    And little recks to find the way to heaven

    By doing deeds of hospitality.

    Besides, his cote, his flocks and bounds of feed

    Are now on sale, and at our sheepcote now,

    By reason of his absence, there is nothing

    That you will feed on; but what is, come see.

    And in my voice most welcome shall you be.

ROSALIND

    What is he that shall buy his flock and pasture?

CORIN

    That young swain that you saw here but
        erewhile,

    That little cares for buying any thing.

ROSALIND

    I pray thee, if it stand with honesty,

    Buy thou the cottage, pasture and the flock,

    And thou shalt have to pay for it of us.

CELIA

And we will mend thy wages. I like this place.

And willingly could waste my time in it.

CORIN

Assuredly the thing is to be sold.

Go with me; if you like upon report

The soil, the profit and this kind of life,

I will your very faithful feeder be

And buy it with your gold right suddenly.

Exeunt

SCENE V. THE FOREST.

Enter AMIENS, JAQUES, and others
SONG

AMIENS

Under the greenwood tree

Who loves to lie with me,

And turn his merry note

Unto the sweet bird's throat,

Come hither, come hither, come hither.

Here shall he see No enemy

But winter and rough weather.

JAQUES

More, more, I prithee, more.

AMIENS

It will make you melancholy, Monsieur Jaques.

JAQUES

I thank it. More, I prithee, more. I can suck melancholy out of a song, as a weasel sucks eggs. More, I prithee, more.

AMIENS

My voice is ragged; I know I cannot please you.

JAQUES

I do not desire you to please me; I do desire you to sing. Come, more; another stanzo. Call you 'em stanzos?

AMIENS

What you will, Monsieur Jaques.

JAQUES

Nay, I care not for their names; they owe me nothing. Will you sing?

AMIENS

More at your request than to please myself.

JAQUES

Well then, if ever I thank any man, I'll thank you; but that they call compliment is like the encounter of two dog-apes, and when a man thanks me heartily, methinks I have given him a penny and he renders me the beggarly thanks. Come, sing; and you that will not, hold your tongues.

AMIENS

Well, I'll end the song. Sirs, cover the while; the Duke will drink under this tree. He hath been all this day to look you.

JAQUES

And I have been all this day to avoid him. He is too disputable for my company. I think of as many matters as he, but I give heaven thanks and make no boast of them. Come, warble, come.

SONG

All together here

Who doth ambition shun
And loves to live i' the sun,
Seeking the food he eats
And pleased with what he gets,
Come hither, come hither, come hither.
Here shall he see
No enemy
But winter and rough weather.

JAQUES

I'll give you a verse to this note that I made yesterday in despite of my invention.

AMIENS

And I'll sing it.

JAQUES

Thus it goes:—

> If it do come to pass
> That any man turn ass,
> Leaving his wealth and ease,
> A stubborn will to please,
> Ducdame, ducdame, ducdame;
> Here shall he see
> Gross fools as he,
> An if he will come to me.

AMIENS

What's that 'ducdame'?

JAQUES

'Tis a Greek invocation, to call fools into a circle. I'll go sleep, if I can; if I cannot, I'll rail against all the first-born of Egypt.

AMIENS

And I'll go seek the Duke; his banquet is prepared.

Exeunt severally

SCENE VI. THE FOREST.

Enter ORLANDO and ADAM

ADAM

Dear master, I can go no further. O, I die for food! Here lie I down, and measure out my grave. Farewell, kind master.

ORLANDO

Why, how now, Adam! no greater heart in thee? Live a little; comfort a little; cheer thyself a little. If this uncouth forest yield any thing savage, I will either be food for it or bring it for food to thee. Thy conceit is nearer death than thy powers. For my sake be comfortable; hold death awhile at the arm's end. I will here be with thee presently; and if I bring thee not something to eat, I will give thee leave to die; but if thou diest before I come, thou art a mocker of my labour. Well said! thou lookest cheerly, and I'll be with thee quickly. Yet thou liest in the bleak air. Come, I will bear thee to some shelter; and thou shalt not die for lack of a dinner, if there live any thing in this desert. Cheerly, good Adam!

Exeunt

SCENE VII. THE FOREST.

A table set out. Enter DUKE SENIOR, AMIENS, and Lords like outlaws

DUKE SENIOR

I think he be transform'd into a beast;
For I can nowhere find him like a man.

FIRST LORD

My lord, he is but even now gone hence;

Here was he merry, hearing of a song.

DUKE SENIOR

If he, compact of jars, grow musical,

We shall have shortly discord in the spheres.

Go, seek him; tell him I would speak with him.

Enter JAQUES

FIRST LORD

He saves my labour by his own approach.

DUKE SENIOR

Why, how now, monsieur! what a life is this,

That your poor friends must woo your company?

What, you look merrily!

JAQUES

A fool, a fool! I met a fool i' the forest,

A motley fool; a miserable world!

As I do live by food, I met a fool

Who laid him down and bask'd him in the sun,

And rail'd on Lady Fortune in good terms,

In good set terms and yet a motley fool.

'Good morrow, fool,' quoth I. 'No, sir,' quoth he,

'Call me not fool till heaven hath sent me fortune.'

And then he drew a dial from his poke,

And, looking on it with lack-lustre eye,

Says very wisely, 'It is ten o'clock;
Thus we may see,' quoth he, 'how the world
wags;
'Tis but an hour ago since it was nine,
And after one hour more 'twill be eleven;
And so, from hour to hour, we ripe and ripe,
And then, from hour to hour, we rot and rot;
And thereby hangs a tale.' When I did hear
The motley fool thus moral on the time,
My lungs began to crow like chanticleer,
That fools should be so deep-contemplative,
And I did laugh sans intermission
An hour by his dial. O noble fool!
A worthy fool! Motley's the only wear.

DUKE SENIOR

What fool is this?

JAQUES

O worthy fool! One that hath been a courtier,
And says, if ladies be but young and fair,
They have the gift to know it; and in his brain,
Which is as dry as the remainder biscuit
After a voyage, he hath strange places cramm'd
With observation, the which he vents
In mangled forms. O that I were a fool!
I am ambitious for a motley coat.

DUKE SENIOR

Thou shalt have one.

JAQUES

    It is my only suit;
    Provided that you weed your better judgments
    Of all opinion that grows rank in them
    That I am wise. I must have liberty
    Withal, as large a charter as the wind,
    To blow on whom I please; for so fools have;
    And they that are most galled with my folly,
    They most must laugh. And why, sir, must they
        so?
    The 'why' is plain as way to parish church:
    He that a fool doth very wisely hit
    Doth very foolishly, although he smart,
    Not to seem senseless of the bob; if not,
    The wise man's folly is anatomized
    Even by the squandering glances of the fool.
    Invest me in my motley; give me leave
    To speak my mind, and I will through and through
    Cleanse the foul body of the infected world,
    If they will patiently receive my medicine.

DUKE SENIOR

    Fie on thee! I can tell what thou wouldst do.

JAQUES

    What, for a counter, would I do but good?

DUKE SENIOR

    Most mischievous foul sin, in chiding sin;
    For thou thyself hast been a libertine,

As sensual as the brutish sting itself;
And all the embossed sores and headed evils,
That thou with licence of free foot hast caught,
Wouldst thou disgorge into the general world.

JAQUES

Why, who cries out on pride,
That can therein tax any private party?
Doth it not flow as hugely as the sea,
Till that the weary very means do ebb?
What woman in the city do I name,
When that I say the city-woman bears
The cost of princes on unworthy shoulders?
Who can come in and say that I mean her,
When such a one as she such is her neighbour?
Or what is he of basest function
That says his bravery is not of my cost,
Thinking that I mean him, but therein suits
His folly to the mettle of my speech?
There then; how then? what then? Let me see
    wherein
My tongue hath wrong'd him: if it do him right,
Then he hath wrong'd himself; if he be free,
Why then my taxing like a wild-goose flies,
Unclaim'd of any man. But who comes here?

Enter ORLANDO, with his sword drawn

ORLANDO

Forbear, and eat no more.

JAQUES

Why, I have eat none yet.

ORLANDO

Nor shalt not, till necessity be served.

JAQUES

Of what kind should this cock come of?

DUKE SENIOR

Art thou thus bolden'd, man, by thy distress,

Or else a rude despiser of good manners,

That in civility thou seem'st so empty?

ORLANDO

You touch'd my vein at first: the thorny point

Of bare distress hath ta'en from me the show

Of smooth civility; yet am I inland bred

And know some nurture. But forbear, I say;

He dies that touches any of this fruit

Till I and my affairs are answered.

JAQUES

An you will not be answered with reason, I must die.

DUKE SENIOR

What would you have? Your gentleness shall force

More than your force move us to gentleness.

ORLANDO

I almost die for food; and let me have it.

DUKE SENIOR

Sit down and feed, and welcome to our table.

ORLANDO

Speak you so gently? Pardon me, I pray you;
I thought that all things had been savage here;
And therefore put I on the countenance
Of stern commandment. But whate'er you are
That in this desert inaccessible,
Under the shade of melancholy boughs,
Lose and neglect the creeping hours of time
If ever you have look'd on better days,
If ever been where bells have knoll'd to church,
If ever sat at any good man's feast,
If ever from your eyelids wiped a tear
And know what 'tis to pity and be pitied,
Let gentleness my strong enforcement be;
In the which hope I blush, and hide my sword.

DUKE SENIOR

True is it that we have seen better days,
And have with holy bell been knoll'd to church
And sat at good men's feasts and wiped our
    eyes
Of drops that sacred pity hath engender'd;
And therefore sit you down in gentleness
And take upon command what help we have
That to your wanting may be minister'd.

ORLANDO

> Then but forbear your food a little while,
> Whiles, like a doe, I go to find my fawn
> And give it food. There is an old poor man,
> Who after me hath many a weary step
> Limp'd in pure love; till he be first sufficed,
> Oppress'd with two weak evils, age and hunger,
> I will not touch a bit.

DUKE SENIOR

> Go find him out,
> And we will nothing waste till you return.

ORLANDO

> I thank ye; and be blest for your good comfort!

> > *Exit*

DUKE SENIOR

> Thou seest we are not all alone unhappy:
> This wide and universal theatre
> Presents more woeful pageants than the scene
> Wherein we play in.

JAQUES

> All the world's a stage,
> And all the men and women merely players;
> They have their exits and their entrances;
> And one man in his time plays many parts,
> His acts being seven ages. At first the infant,
> Mewling and puking in the nurse's arms.
> And then the whining schoolboy, with his satchel

And shining morning face, creeping like snail
Unwillingly to school. And then the lover,
Sighing like furnace, with a woeful ballad
Made to his mistress' eyebrow. Then a soldier,
Full of strange oaths and bearded like the pard,
Jealous in honour, sudden and quick in quarrel,
Seeking the bubble reputation
Even in the cannon's mouth. And then the justice,
In fair round belly with good capon lined,
With eyes severe and beard of formal cut,
Full of wise saws and modern instances;
And so he plays his part. The sixth age shifts
Into the lean and slipper'd pantaloon,
With spectacles on nose and pouch on side,
His youthful hose, well saved, a world too wide
For his shrunk shank; and his big manly voice,
Turning again toward childish treble, pipes
And whistles in his sound. Last scene of all,
That ends this strange eventful history,
Is second childishness and mere oblivion,
Sans teeth, sans eyes, sans taste, sans everything.

Re-enter ORLANDO, with ADAM

DUKE SENIOR

Welcome. Set down your venerable burthen,
And let him feed.

ORLANDO

I thank you most for him.

ADAM

So had you need;

I scarce can speak to thank you for myself.

DUKE SENIOR

Welcome; fall to. I will not trouble you

As yet, to question you about your fortunes.

Give us some music; and, good cousin, sing.

SONG

Blow, blow, thou winter wind.

Thou art not so unkind

As man's ingratitude;

Thy tooth is not so keen,

Because thou art not seen,

Although thy breath be rude.

Heigh-ho! sing, heigh-ho! unto the green holly!

Most friendship is feigning, most loving mere folly.

Then, heigh-ho, the holly!

This life is most jolly.

Freeze, freeze, thou bitter sky,

That dost not bite so nigh

As benefits forgot;

Though thou the waters warp,

Thy sting is not so sharp

As friend remember'd not.

Heigh-ho! sing, etc.

DUKE SENIOR

If that you were the good Sir Rowland's son,
As you have whisper'd faithfully you were,
And as mine eye doth his effigies witness
Most truly limn'd and living in your face,
Be truly welcome hither. I am the Duke
That loved your father. The residue of your
    fortune,
Go to my cave and tell me. Good old man,
Thou art right welcome as thy master is.
Support him by the arm. Give me your hand,
And let me all your fortunes understand.

Exeunt

Act 3

SCENE I. A ROOM IN THE PALACE.

Enter DUKE FREDERICK, Lords, and OLIVER
DUKE FREDERICK

    Not see him since? Sir, sir, that cannot be.
    But were I not the better part made mercy,
    I should not seek an absent argument
    Of my revenge, thou present. But look to it:
    Find out thy brother, wheresoe'er he is;
    Seek him with candle; bring him dead or living
    Within this twelvemonth, or turn thou no more
    To seek a living in our territory.
    Thy lands and all things that thou dost call thine
    Worth seizure do we seize into our hands,
    Till thou canst quit thee by thy brothers mouth
    Of what we think against thee.

OLIVER

>O that your highness knew my heart in this!
>I never loved my brother in my life.

DUKE FREDERICK

>More villain thou. Well, push him out of doors;
>And let my officers of such a nature
>Make an extent upon his house and lands.
>Do this expediently and turn him going.

>>*Exeunt*

SCENE II. THE FOREST.

Enter ORLANDO, with a paper

ORLANDO

>Hang there, my verse, in witness of my love;
>And thou, thrice-crowned queen of night, survey
>With thy chaste eye, from thy pale sphere above,
>Thy huntress' name that my full life doth sway.
>O Rosalind! these trees shall be my books
>And in their barks my thoughts I'll character;
>That every eye which in this forest looks
>Shall see thy virtue witness'd every where.
>Run, run, Orlando; carve on every tree
>The fair, the chaste and unexpressive she.

>>*Exit*

Enter CORIN and TOUCHSTONE

CORIN

And how like you this shepherd's life, Master
Touchstone?

TOUCHSTONE

Truly, shepherd, in respect of itself, it is a good
life, but in respect that it is a shepherd's life, it
is naught. In respect that it is solitary, I like it
very well; but in respect that it is private, it is a
very vile life. Now, in respect it is in the fields,
it pleaseth me well; but in respect it is not in the
court, it is tedious. As is it a spare life, look you,
it fits my humour well; but as there is no more
plenty in it, it goes much against my stomach.
Hast any philosophy in thee, shepherd?

CORIN

No more but that I know the more one sickens
the worse at ease he is; and that he that wants
money, means and content is without three
good friends; that the property of rain is to wet
and fire to burn; that good pasture makes fat
sheep, and that a great cause of the night is lack
of the sun; that he that hath learned no wit by
nature nor art may complain of good breeding
or comes of a very dull kindred.

TOUCHSTONE

Such a one is a natural philosopher. Wast ever
in court, shepherd?

CORIN

No, truly.

TOUCHSTONE

Then thou art damned.

CORIN

Nay, I hope.

TOUCHSTONE

Truly, thou art damned like an ill-roasted egg, all on one side.

CORIN

For not being at court? Your reason.

TOUCHSTONE

Why, if thou never wast at court, thou never sawest good manners; if thou never sawest good manners, then thy manners must be wicked; and wickedness is sin, and sin is damnation. Thou art in a parlous state, shepherd.

CORIN

Not a whit, Touchstone. Those that are good manners at the court are as ridiculous in the country as the behavior of the country is most mockable at the court. You told me you salute not at the court, but you kiss your hands; that courtesy would be uncleanly, if courtiers were shepherds.

TOUCHSTONE

Instance, briefly; come, instance.

CORIN

Why, we are still handling our ewes, and their
fells, you know, are greasy.

TOUCHSTONE

Why, do not your courtier's hands sweat? And
is not the grease of a mutton as wholesome as
the sweat of a man? Shallow, shallow. A better
instance, I say; come.

CORIN

Besides, our hands are hard.

TOUCHSTONE

Your lips will feel them the sooner. Shallow
again. A more sounder instance, come.

CORIN

And they are often tarred over with the
surgery of our sheep; and would you have us
kiss tar? The courtier's hands are perfumed
with civet.

TOUCHSTONE

Most shallow man! thou worms-meat, in
respect of a good piece of flesh indeed! Learn
of the wise, and perpend: civet is of a baser
birth than tar, the very uncleanly flux of a cat.
Mend the instance, shepherd.

CORIN

You have too courtly a wit for me; I'll rest.

TOUCHSTONE

Wilt thou rest damned? God help thee, shallow
man!

God make incision in thee! thou art raw.

CORIN

Sir, I am a true labourer: I earn that I eat, get
that I wear, owe no man hate, envy no man's
happiness, glad of other men's good, content
with my harm, and the greatest of my pride is
to see my ewes graze and my lambs suck.

TOUCHSTONE

That is another simple sin in you, to bring the
ewes and the rams together and to offer to
get your living by the copulation of cattle; to
be bawd to a bell-wether, and to betray a she-
lamb of a twelvemonth to a crooked-pated,
old, cuckoldly ram, out of all reasonable match.
If thou beest not damned for this, the devil
himself will have no shepherds; I cannot see
else how thou shouldst scape.

CORIN

Here comes young Master Ganymede, my new
mistress's brother.

Enter ROSALIND, with a paper, reading

ROSALIND

From the east to western Ind,
No jewel is like Rosalind.

Her worth, being mounted on the wind,
Through all the world bears Rosalind.
All the pictures fairest lined
Are but black to Rosalind.
Let no fair be kept in mind
But the fair of Rosalind.

TOUCHSTONE

I'll rhyme you so eight years together, dinners
and suppers and sleeping-hours excepted. It is
the right butter-women's rank to market.

ROSALIND

Out, fool!

TOUCHSTONE

For a taste:
If a hart do lack a hind,
Let him seek out Rosalind.
If the cat will after kind,
So be sure will Rosalind.
Winter garments must be lined,
So must slender Rosalind.
They that reap must sheaf and bind;
Then to cart with Rosalind.
Sweetest nut hath sourest rind,
Such a nut is Rosalind.
He that sweetest rose will find
Must find love's prick and Rosalind.

This is the very false gallop of verses; why do
you infect yourself with them?

ROSALIND

Peace, you dull fool! I found them on a tree.

TOUCHSTONE

Truly, the tree yields bad fruit.

ROSALIND

I'll graff it with you, and then I shall graff
it with a medlar. Then it will be the earliest
fruit i' the country; for you'll be rotten ere you
be half ripe, and that's the right virtue of the
medlar.

TOUCHSTONE

You have said; but whether wisely or no, let the
forest judge.

Enter CELIA, with a writing

ROSALIND

Peace! Here comes my sister, reading; stand
aside.

CELIA

[*Reads*]

'Why should this a desert be?

For it is unpeopled? No;

Tongues I'll hang on every tree,

That shall civil sayings show.

Some, how brief the life of man

Runs his erring pilgrimage,

That the stretching of a span
Buckles in his sum of age;
Some, of violated vows
'Twixt the souls of friend and friend;
But upon the fairest boughs,
Or at every sentence end,
Will I Rosalinda write,
Teaching all that read to know
The quintessence of every sprite
Heaven would in little show.
Therefore Heaven Nature charged
That one body should be fill'd
With all graces wide-enlarged.
Nature presently distill'd
Helen's cheek, but not her heart,
Cleopatra's majesty,
Atalanta's better part,
Sad Lucretia's modesty.
Thus Rosalind of many parts
By heavenly synod was devised,
Of many faces, eyes and hearts,
To have the touches dearest prized.
Heaven would that she these gifts should have,
And I to live and die her slave.'

ROSALIND

O most gentle pulpiter! What tedious homily
of love have you wearied your parishioners

withal, and never cried 'Have patience, good people!'

CELIA

How now! back, friends! Shepherd, go off a little.

Go with him, sirrah.

TOUCHSTONE

Come, shepherd, let us make an honourable retreat; though not with bag and baggage, yet with scrip and scrippage.

Exeunt CORIN and TOUCHSTONE

CELIA

Didst thou hear these verses?

ROSALIND

O, yes, I heard them all, and more too; for some of them had in them more feet than the verses would bear.

CELIA

That's no matter; the feet might bear the verses.

ROSALIND

Ay, but the feet were lame and could not bear themselves without the verse and therefore stood lamely in the verse.

CELIA

But didst thou hear without wondering how thy name should be hanged and carved upon these trees?

ROSALIND

I was seven of the nine days out of the wonder before you came; for look here what I found on a palm-tree. I was never so be-rhymed since Pythagoras' time, that I was an Irish rat, which I can hardly remember.

CELIA

Trow you who hath done this?

ROSALIND

Is it a man?

CELIA

And a chain, that you once wore, about his neck.

Change you colour?

ROSALIND

I prithee, who?

CELIA

O Lord, Lord! it is a hard matter for friends to meet; but mountains may be removed with earthquakes and so encounter.

ROSALIND

Nay, but who is it?

CELIA

Is it possible?

ROSALIND

Nay, I prithee now with most petitionary vehemence, tell me who it is.

CELIA

O wonderful, wonderful, and most wonderful wonderful! and yet again wonderful, and after that, out of all hooping!

ROSALIND

Good my complexion! dost thou think, though I am caparisoned like a man, I have a doublet and hose in my disposition? One inch of delay more is a South-sea of discovery; I prithee, tell me who is it quickly, and speak apace. I would thou couldst stammer, that thou mightst pour this concealed man out of thy mouth, as wine comes out of a narrow-mouthed bottle, either too much at once, or none at all. I prithee, take the cork out of thy mouth that may drink thy tidings.

CELIA

So you may put a man in your belly.

ROSALIND

Is he of God's making? What manner of man? Is his head worth a hat, or his chin worth a beard?

CELIA

Nay, he hath but a little beard.

ROSALIND

Why, God will send more, if the man will be thankful. Let me stay the growth of his beard, if thou delay me not the knowledge of his chin.

CELIA

It is young Orlando, that tripped up the wrestler's heels and your heart both in an instant.

ROSALIND

Nay, but the devil take mocking!
Speak, sad brow and true maid.

CELIA

I' faith, coz, 'tis he.

ROSALIND

Orlando?

CELIA

Orlando.

ROSALIND

Alas the day! what shall I do with my doublet and hose? What did he when thou sawest him? What said he? How looked he? Wherein went he? What makes him here? Did he ask for me? Where remains he? How parted he with thee? and when shalt thou see him again? Answer me in one word.

CELIA

You must borrow me Gargantua's mouth first; 'tis a word too great for any mouth of this age's size. To say ay and no to these particulars is more than to answer in a catechism.

ROSALIND

But doth he know that I am in this forest and in man's apparel? Looks he as freshly as he did the day he wrestled?

CELIA

It is as easy to count atomies as to resolve the propositions of a lover; but take a taste of my finding him, and relish it with good observance. I found him under a tree, like a dropped acorn.

ROSALIND

It may well be called Jove's tree, when it drops forth such fruit.

CELIA

Give me audience, good madam.

ROSALIND

Proceed.

CELIA

There lay he, stretched along, like a wounded knight.

ROSALIND

Though it be pity to see such a sight, it well becomes the ground.

CELIA

Cry 'holla' to thy tongue, I prithee; it curvets unseasonably. He was furnished like a hunter.

ROSALIND

O, ominous! he comes to kill my heart.

CELIA

I would sing my song without a burden; thou bringest me out of tune.

ROSALIND

Do you not know I am a woman?

When I think, I must speak. Sweet, say on.

CELIA

You bring me out. Soft! comes he not here?

Enter ORLANDO and JAQUES

ROSALIND

'Tis he; slink by, and note him.

JAQUES

I thank you for your company; but, good faith, I had as lief have been myself alone.

ORLANDO

And so had I; but yet, for fashion sake, I thank you too for your society.

JAQUES

God be wi' you; let's meet as little as we can.

ORLANDO

I do desire we may be better strangers.

JAQUES

I pray you, mar no more trees with writing love-songs in their barks.

ORLANDO

I pray you, mar no more of my verses with reading them ill-favouredly.

JAQUES

Rosalind is your love's name?

ORLANDO

Yes, just.

JAQUES

I do not like her name.

ORLANDO

There was no thought of pleasing you when she was christened.

JAQUES

What stature is she of?

ORLANDO

Just as high as my heart.

JAQUES

You are full of pretty answers. Have you not been acquainted with goldsmiths' wives, and conned them out of rings?

ORLANDO

Not so; but I answer you right painted cloth, from whence you have studied your questions.

JAQUES

You have a nimble wit; I think 'twas made of Atalanta's heels. Will you sit down with me?

and we two will rail against our mistress the world and all our misery.

ORLANDO

I will chide no breather in the world but myself, against whom I know most faults.

JAQUES

The worst fault you have is to be in love.

ORLANDO

'Tis a fault I will not change for your best virtue. I am weary of you.

JAQUES

By my troth, I was seeking for a fool when I found you.

ORLANDO

He is drowned in the brook; look but in, and you shall see him.

JAQUES

There I shall see mine own figure.

ORLANDO

Which I take to be either a fool or a cipher.

JAQUES

I'll tarry no longer with you; farewell, good Signior Love.

ORLANDO

I am glad of your departure; adieu, good Monsieur Melancholy.

Exit JAQUES

ROSALIND

[*Aside to CELIA*] I will speak to him, like a saucy lackey and under that habit play the knave with him. Do you hear, forester?

ORLANDO

Very well; what would you?

ROSALIND

I pray you, what is't o'clock?

ORLANDO

You should ask me what time o' day; there's no clock in the forest.

ROSALIND

Then there is no true lover in the forest; else sighing every minute and groaning every hour would detect the lazy foot of Time as well as a clock.

ORLANDO

And why not the swift foot of Time?
Had not that been as proper?

ROSALIND

By no means, sir. Time travels in divers paces with divers persons. I'll tell you who Time ambles withal, who Time trots withal, who Time gallops withal and who he stands still withal.

ORLANDO

I prithee, who doth he trot withal?

ROSALIND

Marry, he trots hard with a young maid between the contract of her marriage and the day it is solemnized; if the interim be but a se'nnight, Time's pace is so hard that it seems the length of seven year.

ORLANDO

Who ambles Time withal?

ROSALIND

With a priest that lacks Latin and a rich man that hath not the gout, for the one sleeps easily because he cannot study, and the other lives merrily because he feels no pain, the one lacking the burden of lean and wasteful learning, the other knowing no burden of heavy tedious penury; these Time ambles withal.

ORLANDO

Who doth he gallop withal?

ROSALIND

With a thief to the gallows, for though he go as softly as foot can fall, he thinks himself too soon there.

ORLANDO

Who stays it still withal?

ROSALIND

With lawyers in the vacation, for they sleep between term and term and then they perceive not how Time moves.

ORLANDO

Where dwell you, pretty youth?

ROSALIND

With this shepherdess, my sister; here in the skirts of the forest, like fringe upon a petticoat.

ORLANDO

Are you native of this place?

ROSALIND

As the cony that you see dwell where she is kindled.

ORLANDO

Your accent is something finer than you could purchase in so removed a dwelling.

ROSALIND

I have been told so of many; but indeed an old religious uncle of mine taught me to speak, who was in his youth an inland man; one that knew courtship too well, for there he fell in love. I have heard him read many lectures against it, and I thank God I am not a woman, to be touched with so many giddy offences as he hath generally taxed their whole sex withal.

ORLANDO

Can you remember any of the principal evils
that he laid to the charge of women?

ROSALIND

There were none principal; they were all like
one another as half-pence are, every one fault
seeming monstrous till his fellow fault came
to match it.

ORLANDO

I prithee, recount some of them.

ROSALIND

No, I will not cast away my physic but on
those that are sick. There is a man haunts
the forest, that abuses our young plants with
carving 'Rosalind' on their barks; hangs odes
upon hawthorns and elegies on brambles, all,
forsooth, deifying the name of Rosalind. If I
could meet that fancy-monger I would give
him some good counsel, for he seems to have
the quotidian of love upon him.

ORLANDO

I am he that is so love-shaked; I pray you tell
me your remedy.

ROSALIND

There is none of my uncle's marks upon you;
he taught me how to know a man in love; in

which cage of rushes I am sure you are not prisoner.

ORLANDO

What were his marks?

ROSALIND

A lean cheek, which you have not, a blue eye and sunken, which you have not, an unquestionable spirit, which you have not, a beard neglected, which you have not; but I pardon you for that, for simply your having in beard is a younger brother's revenue. Then your hose should be ungartered, your bonnet unbanded, your sleeve unbuttoned, your shoe untied and every thing about you demonstrating a careless desolation; but you are no such man; you are rather point-device in your accoutrements as loving yourself than seeming the lover of any other.

ORLANDO

Fair youth, I would I could make thee believe I love.

ROSALIND

Me believe it! you may as soon make her that you love believe it; which, I warrant, she is apter to do than to confess she does. That is one of the points in the which women still give the lie to their consciences. But, in good sooth, are you he that hangs the verses on the trees, wherein Rosalind is so admired?

ORLANDO

I swear to thee, youth, by the white hand of Rosalind, I am that he, that unfortunate he.

ROSALIND

But are you so much in love as your rhymes speak?

ORLANDO

Neither rhyme nor reason can express how much.

ROSALIND

Love is merely a madness, and, I tell you, deserves as well a dark house and a whip as madmen do; and the reason why they are not so punished and cured is, that the lunacy is so ordinary that the whippers are in love too. Yet I profess curing it by counsel.

ORLANDO

Did you ever cure any so?

ROSALIND

Yes, one, and in this manner. He was to imagine me his love, his mistress; and I set him every day to woo me; at which time would I, being but a moonish youth, grieve, be effeminate, changeable, longing and liking, proud, fantastical, apish, shallow, inconstant, full of tears, full of smiles, for every passion something and for no passion truly any thing, as boys and women are for the most part cattle of this colour; would now like him, now loathe him; then entertain him, then forswear him; now weep for him, then spit at him; that I drave my suitor from his mad humour of love to a living humour of madness; which was, to forswear the full stream of the world, and to live in a nook merely monastic. And thus I cured him; and this way will I take upon me to wash your liver as clean as a sound sheep's heart, that there shall not be one spot of love in't.

ORLANDO

I would not be cured, youth.

ROSALIND

I would cure you, if you would but call me Rosalind and come every day to my cote and woo me.

ORLANDO

Now, by the faith of my love, I will. Tell me where it is.

ROSALIND

Go with me to it and I'll show it you and by the way you shall tell me where in the forest you live. Will you go?

ORLANDO

With all my heart, good youth.

ROSALIND

Nay you must call me Rosalind. Come, sister, will you go?

Exeunt

SCENE III. THE FOREST.

Enter TOUCHSTONE and AUDREY; JAQUES behind

TOUCHSTONE

Come apace, good Audrey; I will fetch up your goats, Audrey. And how, Audrey, am I the man yet? Doth my simple feature content you?

AUDREY

Your features! Lord warrant us! what features!

TOUCHSTONE

I am here with thee and thy goats, as the most capricious poet, honest Ovid, was among the Goths.

JAQUES

[*Aside*] O knowledge ill-inhabited, worse than Jove in a thatched house!

TOUCHSTONE

When a man's verses cannot be understood, nor a man's good wit seconded with the forward child Understanding, it strikes a man more dead than a great reckoning in a little room. Truly, I would the gods had made thee poetical.

AUDREY

I do not know what 'poetical' is. Is it honest in deed and word? Is it a true thing?

TOUCHSTONE

No, truly; for the truest poetry is the most feigning; and lovers are given to poetry, and what they swear in poetry may be said as lovers they do feign.

AUDREY

Do you wish then that the gods had made me poetical?

TOUCHSTONE

I do, truly; for thou swearest to me thou art honest; now, if thou wert a poet, I might have some hope thou didst feign.

AUDREY

Would you not have me honest?

TOUCHSTONE

No, truly, unless thou wert hard-favoured; for honesty coupled to beauty is to have honey a sauce to sugar.

JAQUES

[*Aside*] A material fool!

AUDREY

Well, I am not fair; and therefore I pray the gods make me honest.

TOUCHSTONE

Truly, and to cast away honesty upon a foul slut were to put good meat into an unclean dish.

AUDREY

I am not a slut, though I thank the gods I am foul.

TOUCHSTONE

Well, praised be the gods for thy foulness; sluttishness may come hereafter. But be it as it may be, I will marry thee, and to that end I have been with Sir Oliver Martext, the vicar of the next village, who hath promised to meet me in this place of the forest and to couple us.

JAQUES

[*Aside*] I would fain see this meeting.

AUDREY

Well, the gods give us joy!

TOUCHSTONE

Amen. A man may, if he were of a fearful heart, stagger in this attempt; for here we have no temple but the wood, no assembly but horn-beasts. But what though? Courage! As horns are odious, they are necessary. It is said, 'many a man knows no end of his goods.' Right! many a man has good horns, and knows no end of them. Well, that is the dowry of his wife; 'tis none of his own getting. Horns? Even so. Poor men alone? No, no; the noblest deer hath them as huge as the rascal. Is the single man therefore blessed? No; as a walled town is more worthier than a village, so is the forehead of a married man more honourable than the bare brow of a bachelor; and by how much defence is better than no skill, by so much is a horn more precious than to want. Here comes Sir Oliver.

Enter SIR OLIVER MARTEXT

Sir Oliver Martext, you are well met. Will you dispatch us here under this tree, or shall we go with you to your chapel?

SIR OLIVER MARTEXT

Is there none here to give the woman?

TOUCHSTONE

I will not take her on gift of any man.

SIR OLIVER MARTEXT

Truly, she must be given, or the marriage is not lawful.

JAQUES

[*Advancing*] Proceed, proceed I'll give her.

TOUCHSTONE

Good even, good Master What-ye-call't; how do you, sir? You are very well met. God 'ild you for your last company. I am very glad to see you. Even a toy in hand here, sir. Nay, pray be covered.

JAQUES

Will you be married, motley?

TOUCHSTONE

As the ox hath his bow, sir, the horse his curb and the falcon her bells, so man hath his desires; and as pigeons bill, so wedlock would be nibbling.

JAQUES

And will you, being a man of your breeding, be married under a bush like a beggar? Get you to church, and have a good priest that can tell you what marriage is; this fellow will but join you together as they join wainscot; then one of you will prove a shrunk panel and, like green timber, warp, warp.

TOUCHSTONE

[*Aside*] I am not in the mind but I were better to be married of him than of another; for he is not like to marry me well; and not being well married, it will be a good excuse for me hereafter to leave my wife.

JAQUES

Go thou with me, and let me counsel thee.

TOUCHSTONE

Come, sweet Audrey;

We must be married, or we must live in bawdry.

Farewell, good Master Oliver. Not—

O sweet Oliver,

O brave Oliver,

Leave me not behind thee. But—

Wind away,

Begone, I say,

I will not to wedding with thee.

Exeunt JAQUES, TOUCHSTONE
and AUDREY

SIR OLIVER MARTEXT

'Tis no matter; ne'er a fantastical knave of them all shall flout me out of my calling.

Exit

SCENE IV. THE FOREST.

Enter ROSALIND and CELIA

ROSALIND

Never talk to me; I will weep.

CELIA

Do, I prithee; but yet have the grace to consider that tears do not become a man.

ROSALIND

But have I not cause to weep?

CELIA

As good cause as one would desire; therefore weep.

ROSALIND

His very hair is of the dissembling colour.

CELIA

Something browner than Judas's marry, his kisses are Judas's own children.

ROSALIND

I' faith, his hair is of a good colour.

CELIA

An excellent colour: your chestnut was ever the only colour.

ROSALIND

And his kissing is as full of sanctity as the touch of holy bread.

CELIA

He hath bought a pair of cast lips of Diana. A nun of winter's sisterhood kisses not more religiously; the very ice of chastity is in them.

ROSALIND

But why did he swear he would come this morning, and comes not?

CELIA

Nay, certainly, there is no truth in him.

ROSALIND

Do you think so?

CELIA

Yes; I think he is not a pick-purse nor a horse-stealer, but for his verity in love, I do think him as concave as a covered goblet or a worm-eaten nut.

ROSALIND

Not true in love?

CELIA

Yes, when he is in; but I think he is not in.

ROSALIND

You have heard him swear downright he was.

CELIA

'Was' is not 'is'; besides, the oath of a lover is no stronger than the word of a tapster; they are both the confirmer of false reckonings. He attends here in the forest on the Duke your father.

ROSALIND

I met the Duke yesterday and had much question with him. He asked me of what parentage I was; I told him, of as good as he; so he laughed and let me go. But what talk we of fathers, when there is such a man as Orlando?

CELIA

O, that's a brave man! he writes brave verses, speaks brave words, swears brave oaths and breaks them bravely, quite traverse, athwart

the heart of his lover; as a puisny tilter, that
spurs his horse but on one side, breaks his staff
like a noble goose. But all's brave that youth
mounts and folly guides. Who comes here?

Enter CORIN

CORIN

Mistress and master, you have oft inquired
After the shepherd that complain'd of love,
Who you saw sitting by me on the turf,
Praising the proud disdainful shepherdess
That was his mistress.

CELIA

Well, and what of him?

CORIN

If you will see a pageant truly play'd,
Between the pale complexion of true love
And the red glow of scorn and proud disdain,
Go hence a little and I shall conduct you,
If you will mark it.

ROSALIND

O, come, let us remove!
The sight of lovers feedeth those in love.
Bring us to this sight, and you shall say
I'll prove a busy actor in their play.

Exeunt

SCENE V. ANOTHER PART OF THE

FOREST.

Enter SILVIUS and PHEBE
SILVIUS

>Sweet Phebe, do not scorn me; do not, Phebe;
>Say that you love me not, but say not so
>In bitterness. The common executioner,
>Whose heart the accustom'd sight of death makes hard,
>Falls not the axe upon the humbled neck
>But first begs pardon. Will you sterner be
>Than he that dies and lives by bloody drops?

Enter ROSALIND, CELIA, and CORIN, behind
PHEBE

>I would not be thy executioner;
>I fly thee, for I would not injure thee.
>Thou tell'st me there is murder in mine eye.
>'Tis pretty, sure, and very probable,
>That eyes, that are the frail'st and softest things,
>Who shut their coward gates on atomies,
>Should be call'd tyrants, butchers, murderers!
>Now I do frown on thee with all my heart;
>And if mine eyes can wound, now let them kill thee.
>Now counterfeit to swoon; why now fall down;
>Or if thou canst not, O, for shame, for shame,
>Lie not, to say mine eyes are murderers!

Now show the wound mine eye hath made in
thee.

Scratch thee but with a pin, and there remains

Some scar of it; lean but upon a rush,

The cicatrice and capable impressure

Thy palm some moment keeps; but now mine
eyes,

Which I have darted at thee, hurt thee not,

Nor, I am sure, there is no force in eyes

That can do hurt.

SILVIUS

O dear Phebe,

If ever, as that ever may be near,

You meet in some fresh cheek the power of
fancy,

Then shall you know the wounds invisible

That love's keen arrows make.

PHEBE

But till that time

Come not thou near me; and when that time
comes,

Afflict me with thy mocks, pity me not;

As till that time I shall not pity thee.

ROSALIND

[*Advancing*] And why, I pray you?

Who might be your mother,

That you insult, exult, and all at once,

Over the wretched? What though you have no
    beauty—
As, by my faith, I see no more in you
Than without candle may go dark to bed—
Must you be therefore proud and pitiless?
Why, what means this? Why do you look on
    me?
I see no more in you than in the ordinary
Of nature's sale-work. 'Od's my little life,
I think she means to tangle my eyes too!
No, faith, proud mistress, hope not after it;
'Tis not your inky brows, your black silk hair,
Your bugle eyeballs, nor your cheek of cream,
That can entame my spirits to your worship.
You foolish shepherd, wherefore do you follow
    her,
Like foggy south puffing with wind and rain?
You are a thousand times a properer man
Than she a woman. 'Tis such fools as you
That makes the world full of ill-favour'd children.
'Tis not her glass, but you, that flatters her;
And out of you she sees herself more proper
Than any of her lineaments can show her.
But, mistress, know yourself. Down on your
    knees,
And thank heaven, fasting, for a good man's
    love;

For I must tell you friendly in your ear,
Sell when you can; you are not for all markets.
Cry the man mercy; love him; take his offer;
Foul is most foul, being foul to be a scoffer.
So take her to thee, shepherd. Fare you well.

PHEBE

Sweet youth, I pray you, chide a year together;
I had rather hear you chide than this man woo.

ROSALIND

He's fallen in love with your foulness and she'll
fall in love with my anger. If it be so, as fast
as she answers thee with frowning looks, I'll
sauce her with bitter words. Why look you so
upon me?

PHEBE

For no ill will I bear you.

ROSALIND

I pray you, do not fall in love with me,
For I am falser than vows made in wine;
Besides, I like you not. If you will know my
house,
'Tis at the tuft of olives here hard by.
Will you go, sister? Shepherd, ply her hard.
Come, sister. Shepherdess, look on him better,
And be not proud; though all the world could
see,
None could be so abused in sight as he.

Come, to our flock.

Exeunt ROSALIND, CELIA
and CORIN

PHEBE

Dead Shepherd, now I find thy saw of might,
'Who ever loved that loved not at first sight?'

SILVIUS

Sweet Phebe—

PHEBE

Ha, what say'st thou, Silvius?

SILVIUS

Sweet Phebe, pity me.

PHEBE

Why, I am sorry for thee, gentle Silvius.

SILVIUS

Wherever sorrow is, relief would be.

If you do sorrow at my grief in love,

By giving love your sorrow and my grief

Were both extermined.

PHEBE

Thou hast my love; is not that neighbourly?

SILVIUS

I would have you.

PHEBE

Why, that were covetousness.

Silvius, the time was that I hated thee,

And yet it is not that I bear thee love;

But since that thou canst talk of love so well,
Thy company, which erst was irksome to me,
I will endure, and I'll employ thee too.
But do not look for further recompense
Than thine own gladness that thou art employ'd.

SILVIUS

So holy and so perfect is my love,
And I in such a poverty of grace,
That I shall think it a most plenteous crop
To glean the broken ears after the man
That the main harvest reaps; loose now and
then
A scatter'd smile, and that I'll live upon.

PHEBE

Know'st now the youth that spoke to me
erewhile?

SILVIUS

Not very well, but I have met him oft;
And he hath bought the cottage and the bounds
That the old carlot once was master of.

PHEBE

Think not I love him, though I ask for him;
'Tis but a peevish boy; yet he talks well;
But what care I for words? Yet words do well
When he that speaks them pleases those that
hear.
It is a pretty youth—not very pretty;

But, sure, he's proud, and yet his pride becomes
    him.
He'll make a proper man. The best thing in him
Is his complexion; and faster than his tongue
Did make offence his eye did heal it up.
He is not very tall; yet for his years he's tall;
His leg is but so-so; and yet 'tis well.
There was a pretty redness in his lip,
A little riper and more lusty red
Than that mix'd in his cheek; 'twas just the
    difference
Between the constant red and mingled damask.
There be some women, Silvius, had they mark'd
    him
In parcels as I did, would have gone near
To fall in love with him; but, for my part,
I love him not nor hate him not; and yet
I have more cause to hate him than to love him;
For what had he to do to chide at me?
He said mine eyes were black and my hair black,
And, now I am remember'd, scorn'd at me.
I marvel why I answer'd not again;
But that's all one; omittance is no quittance.
I'll write to him a very taunting letter,
And thou shalt bear it; wilt thou, Silvius?

SILVIUS
    Phebe, with all my heart.

PHEBE
    I'll write it straight;
    The matter's in my head and in my heart;
    I will be bitter with him and passing short.
    Go with me, Silvius.

                          Exeunt

Act 4

SCENE I. THE FOREST.

Enter ROSALIND, CELIA, and JAQUES

JAQUES

I prithee, pretty youth, let me be better acquainted with thee.

ROSALIND

They say you are a melancholy fellow.

JAQUES

I am so; I do love it better than laughing.

ROSALIND

Those that are in extremity of either are abominable fellows and betray themselves to every modern censure worse than drunkards.

JAQUES

Why, 'tis good to be sad and say nothing.

ROSALIND

Why then, 'tis good to be a post.

JAQUES

I have neither the scholar's melancholy, which is emulation, nor the musician's, which is fantastical, nor the courtier's, which is proud, nor the soldier's, which is ambitious, nor the lawyer's, which is politic, nor the lady's, which is nice, nor the lover's, which is all these; but it is a melancholy of mine own, compounded of many simples, extracted from many objects, and indeed the sundry's contemplation of my travels, in which my often rumination wraps me m a most humorous sadness.

ROSALIND

A traveller! By my faith, you have great reason to be sad. I fear you have sold your own lands to see other men's; then, to have seen much and to have nothing, is to have rich eyes and poor hands.

JAQUES

Yes, I have gained my experience.

ROSALIND

And your experience makes you sad. I had rather have a fool to make me merry than experience to make me sad; and to travel for it too!

Enter ORLANDO

ORLANDO

Good day and happiness, dear Rosalind!

JAQUES

Nay, then, God be wi' you, an you talk in blank
verse.

Exit

ROSALIND

Farewell, Monsieur Traveller; look you lisp and
wear strange suits, disable all the benefits of
your own country, be out of love with your
nativity and almost chide God for making you
that countenance you are, or I will scarce think
you have swam in a gondola. Why, how now,
Orlando! where have you been all this while?
You a lover! An you serve me such another
trick, never come in my sight more.

ORLANDO

My fair Rosalind, I come within an hour of my
promise.

ROSALIND

Break an hour's promise in love! He that will
divide a minute into a thousand parts and break
but a part of the thousandth part of a minute
in the affairs of love, it may be said of him that
Cupid hath clapped him o' the shoulder, but
I'll warrant him heart-whole.

ORLANDO

Pardon me, dear Rosalind.

ROSALIND

Nay, an you be so tardy, come no more in my sight. I had as lief be wooed of a snail.

ORLANDO

Of a snail?

ROSALIND

Ay, of a snail; for though he comes slowly, he carries his house on his head; a better jointure, I think, than you make a woman; besides he brings his destiny with him.

ORLANDO

What's that?

ROSALIND

Why, horns, which such as you are fain to be beholding to your wives for; but he comes armed in his fortune and prevents the slander of his wife.

ORLANDO

Virtue is no horn-maker; and my Rosalind is virtuous.

ROSALIND

And I am your Rosalind.

CELIA

It pleases him to call you so; but he hath a Rosalind of a better leer than you.

ROSALIND

Come, woo me, woo me, for now I am in a holiday humour and like enough to consent. What would you say to me now, an I were your very very Rosalind?

ORLANDO

I would kiss before I spoke.

ROSALIND

Nay, you were better speak first, and when you were gravelled for lack of matter, you might take occasion to kiss. Very good orators, when they are out, they will spit; and for lovers lacking—God warn us!—matter, the cleanliest shift is to kiss.

ORLANDO

How if the kiss be denied?

ROSALIND

Then she puts you to entreaty, and there begins new matter.

ORLANDO

Who could be out, being before his beloved mistress?

ROSALIND

Marry, that should you, if I were your mistress, or I should think my honesty ranker than my wit.

ORLANDO

What, of my suit?

ROSALIND

Not out of your apparel, and yet out of your suit. Am not I your Rosalind?

ORLANDO

I take some joy to say you are, because I would be talking of her.

ROSALIND

Well in her person I say I will not have you.

ORLANDO

Then in mine own person I die.

ROSALIND

No, faith, die by attorney. The poor world is almost six thousand years old, and in all this time there was not any man died in his own person, videlicet, in a love-cause. Troilus had his brains dashed out with a Grecian club; yet he did what he could to die before, and he is one of the patterns of love. Leander, he would have lived many a fair year, though Hero had turned nun, if it had not been for a hot midsummer night; for, good youth, he went but forth to wash him in the Hellespont and being taken with the cramp was drowned and the foolish coroners of that age found it was 'Hero of Sestos.' But these are all lies: men have died from time to time and worms have eaten them, but not for love.

ORLANDO

I would not have my right Rosalind of this mind, for, I protest, her frown might kill me.

ROSALIND

By this hand, it will not kill a fly. But come, now I will be your Rosalind in a more coming-on disposition, and ask me what you will. I will grant it.

ORLANDO

Then love me, Rosalind.

ROSALIND

Yes, faith, will I, Fridays and Saturdays and all.

ORLANDO

And wilt thou have me?

ROSALIND

Ay, and twenty such.

ORLANDO

What sayest thou?

ROSALIND

Are you not good?

ORLANDO

I hope so.

ROSALIND

Why then, can one desire too much of a good thing?

Come, sister, you shall be the priest and marry us.

Give me your hand, Orlando. What do you say,
    sister?

ORLANDO

Pray thee, marry us.

CELIA

I cannot say the words.

ROSALIND

You must begin, 'Will you, Orlando—'
    CELIA Go to. Will you, Orlando, have to wife
    this Rosalind?

ORLANDO

I will.

ROSALIND

Ay, but when?

ORLANDO

Why now; as fast as she can marry us.

ROSALIND

Then you must say 'I take thee, Rosalind, for
wife.'

ORLANDO

I take thee, Rosalind, for wife.

ROSALIND

I might ask you for your commission; but I do
take thee, Orlando, for my husband. There's
a girl goes before the priest; and certainly a
woman's thought runs before her actions.

ORLANDO

So do all thoughts; they are winged.

ROSALIND

Now tell me how long you would have her after you have possessed her.

ORLANDO

For ever and a day.

ROSALIND

Say 'a day,' without the 'ever.' No, no, Orlando; men are April when they woo, December when they wed: maids are May when they are maids, but the sky changes when they are wives. I will be more jealous of thee than a Barbary cock-pigeon over his hen, more clamorous than a parrot against rain, more new-fangled than an ape, more giddy in my desires than a monkey. I will weep for nothing, like Diana in the fountain, and I will do that when you are disposed to be merry; I will laugh like a hyen, and that when thou art inclined to sleep.

ORLANDO

But will my Rosalind do so?

ROSALIND

By my life, she will do as I do.

ORLANDO

O, but she is wise.

ROSALIND

Or else she could not have the wit to do this. The wiser, the waywarder. Make the doors upon a woman's wit and it will out at the casement; shut that and 'twill out at the keyhole; stop that, 'twill fly with the smoke out at the chimney.

ORLANDO

A man that had a wife with such a wit, he might say 'Wit, whither wilt?'

ROSALIND

Nay, you might keep that cheque for it till you met your wife's wit going to your neighbour's bed.

ORLANDO

And what wit could wit have to excuse that?

ROSALIND

Marry, to say she came to seek you there. You shall never take her without her answer, unless you take her without her tongue. O, that woman that cannot make her fault her husband's occasion, let her never nurse her child herself, for she will breed it like a fool!

ORLANDO

For these two hours, Rosalind, I will leave thee.

ROSALIND

Alas! dear love, I cannot lack thee two hours.

ORLANDO

I must attend the Duke at dinner; by two o'clock I will be with thee again.

ROSALIND

Ay, go your ways, go your ways; I knew what you would prove; my friends told me as much, and I thought no less. That flattering tongue of yours won me. 'Tis but one cast away, and so, come, death! Two o'clock is your hour?

ORLANDO

Ay, sweet Rosalind.

ROSALIND

By my troth, and in good earnest, and so God mend me, and by all pretty oaths that are not dangerous, if you break one jot of your promise or come one minute behind your hour, I will think you the most pathetical break-promise and the most hollow lover and the most unworthy of her you call Rosalind that may be chosen out of the gross band of the unfaithful. therefore beware my censure and keep your promise.

ORLANDO

With no less religion than if thou wert indeed my Rosalind; so adieu.

ROSALIND

Well, Time is the old justice that examines all such offenders, and let Time try. Adieu.

Exit ORLANDO

CELIA

You have simply misused our sex in your love-prate. We must have your doublet and hose plucked over your head, and show the world what the bird hath done to her own nest.

ROSALIND

O coz, coz, coz, my pretty little coz, that thou didst know how many fathom deep I am in love! But it cannot be sounded; my affection hath an unknown bottom, like the bay of Portugal.

CELIA

Or rather, bottomless, that as fast as you pour affection in, it runs out.

ROSALIND

No, that same wicked bastard of Venus that was begot of thought, conceived of spleen and born of madness, that blind rascally boy that abuses every one's eyes because his own are out, let him be judge how deep I am in love. I'll tell thee, Aliena, I cannot be out of the sight of Orlando. I'll go find a shadow and sigh till he come.

CELIA

    And I'll sleep.

Exeunt

SCENE II. THE FOREST.

Enter JAQUES, Lords, and Foresters

JAQUES

    Which is he that killed the deer?

LORD

    Sir, it was I.

JAQUES

    Let's present him to the Duke, like a Roman conqueror; and it would do well to set the deer's horns upon his head, for a branch of victory. Have you no song, forester, for this purpose?

LORD

    Yes, sir.

JAQUES

    Sing it; 'tis no matter how it be in tune, so it make noise enough.

SONG

    What shall he have that kill'd the deer?

      His leather skin and horns to wear.

        Then sing him home;

        The rest shall bear this burden

Take thou no scorn to wear the horn;
It was a crest ere thou wast born.
Thy father's father wore it,
And thy father bore it.
The horn, the horn, the lusty horn
Is not a thing to laugh to scorn.

Exeunt

SCENE III. THE FOREST.

Enter ROSALIND and CELIA

ROSALIND

How say you now? Is it not past two o'clock?
And here much Orlando!

CELIA

I warrant you, with pure love and troubled
brain, he hath ta'en his bow and arrows and
is gone forth to sleep. Look, who comes here.

Enter SILVIUS

SILVIUS

My errand is to you, fair youth;
My gentle Phebe bid me give you this.
I know not the contents; but, as I guess
By the stern brow and waspish action
Which she did use as she was writing of it,
It bears an angry tenor. Pardon me,
I am but as a guiltless messenger.

ROSALIND

> Patience herself would startle at this letter
> And play the swaggerer; bear this, bear all.
> She says I am not fair, that I lack manners;
> She calls me proud, and that she could not
> love me,
> Were man as rare as phoenix. 'Od's my will!
> Her love is not the hare that I do hunt;
> Why writes she so to me? Well, shepherd, well,
> This is a letter of your own device.

SILVIUS

> No, I protest, I know not the contents; Phebe
> did write it.

ROSALIND

> Come, come, you are a fool
> And turn'd into the extremity of love.
> I saw her hand; she has a leathern hand.
> A freestone-colour'd hand; I verily did think
> That her old gloves were on, but 'twas her hands;
> She has a huswife's hand; but that's no matter.
> I say she never did invent this letter;
> This is a man's invention and his hand.

SILVIUS

> Sure, it is hers.

ROSALIND

> Why, 'tis a boisterous and a cruel style.
> A style for-challengers; why, she defies me,

Like Turk to Christian. Women's gentle brain
Could not drop forth such giant-rude invention
Such Ethiope words, blacker in their effect
Than in their countenance. Will you hear the
letter?

SILVIUS

So please you, for I never heard it yet;
Yet heard too much of Phebe's cruelty.

ROSALIND

She Phebes me: mark how the tyrant writes.
[*Reads*]
Art thou god to shepherd turn'd,
That a maiden's heart hath burn'd?
Can a woman rail thus?

SILVIUS

Call you this railing?

ROSALIND

[*Reads*]
'Why, thy godhead laid apart,
Warr'st thou with a woman's heart?'
Did you ever hear such railing?
'Whiles the eye of man did woo me,
That could do no vengeance to me.'
Meaning me a beast.
'If the scorn of your bright eyne
Have power to raise such love in mine,
Alack, in me what strange effect

Would they work in mild aspect!
Whiles you chid me, I did love;
How then might your prayers move!
He that brings this love to thee
Little knows this love in me;
And by him seal up thy mind;
Whether that thy youth and kind
Will the faithful offer take
Of me and all that I can make;
Or else by him my love deny,
And then I'll study how to die.'

SILVIUS

Call you this chiding?

CELIA

Alas, poor shepherd!

ROSALIND

Do you pity him? No, he deserves no pity. Wilt
thou love such a woman? What, to make thee
an instrument and play false strains upon thee!
Not to be endured! Well, go your way to her,
for I see love hath made thee a tame snake, and
say this to her: that if she love me, I charge her
to love thee; if she will not, I will never have
her unless thou entreat for her. If you be a true
lover, hence, and not a word; for here comes
more company.

Exit SILVIUS

Enter OLIVER

OLIVER

Good morrow, fair ones; pray you, if you know,
Where in the purlieus of this forest stands
A sheep-cote fenced about with olive trees?

CELIA

West of this place, down in the neighbour
bottom.
The rank of osiers by the murmuring stream
Left on your right hand brings you to the place.
But at this hour the house doth keep itself;
There's none within.

OLIVER

If that an eye may profit by a tongue,
Then should I know you by description;
Such garments and such years: 'The boy is fair,
Of female favour, and bestows himself
Like a ripe sister; the woman low
And browner than her brother.' Are not you
The owner of the house I did inquire for?

CELIA

It is no boast, being ask'd, to say we are.

OLIVER

Orlando doth commend him to you both,
And to that youth he calls his Rosalind
He sends this bloody napkin. Are you he?

ROSALIND

    I am. What must we understand by this?

OLIVER

    Some of my shame; if you will know of me

    What man I am, and how, and why, and where

    This handkercher was stain'd.

CELIA

    I pray you, tell it.

OLIVER

    When last the young Orlando parted from you

    He left a promise to return again

    Within an hour, and pacing through the forest,

    Chewing the food of sweet and bitter fancy,

    Lo, what befell! he threw his eye aside,

    And mark what object did present itself.

    Under an oak, whose boughs were moss'd with

        age

    And high top bald with dry antiquity,

    A wretched ragged man, o'ergrown with hair,

    Lay sleeping on his back. About his neck

    A green and gilded snake had wreathed itself,

    Who with her head nimble in threats approach'd

    The opening of his mouth; but suddenly,

    Seeing Orlando, it unlink'd itself,

    And with indented glides did slip away

    Into a bush; under which bush's shade

A lioness, with udders all drawn dry,
Lay couching, head on ground, with catlike
    watch,
When that the sleeping man should stir; for 'tis
The royal disposition of that beast
To prey on nothing that doth seem as dead.
This seen, Orlando did approach the man
And found it was his brother, his elder brother.

CELIA

O, I have heard him speak of that same brother;
And he did render him the most unnatural
That lived amongst men.

OLIVER

And well he might so do,
For well I know he was unnatural.

ROSALIND

But, to Orlando: did he leave him there,
Food to the suck'd and hungry lioness?

OLIVER

Twice did he turn his back and purposed so;
But kindness, nobler ever than revenge,
And nature, stronger than his just occasion,
Made him give battle to the lioness,
Who quickly fell before him; in which hurtling
From miserable slumber I awaked.

CELIA

Are you his brother?

ROSALIND

Wast you he rescued?

CELIA

Was't you that did so oft contrive to kill him?

OLIVER

'Twas I; but 'tis not I. I do not shame

To tell you what I was, since my conversion

So sweetly tastes, being the thing I am.

ROSALIND

But, for the bloody napkin?

OLIVER

By and by.

When from the first to last betwixt us two

Tears our recountments had most kindly
     bathed,

As how I came into that desert place—

In brief, he led me to the gentle Duke,

Who gave me fresh array and entertainment,

Committing me unto my brother's love;

Who led me instantly unto his cave,

There stripp'd himself, and here upon his arm

The lioness had torn some flesh away,

Which all this while had bled; and now he fainted

And cried, in fainting, upon Rosalind.

Brief, I recover'd him, bound up his wound;

And, after some small space, being strong at
     heart,

He sent me hither, stranger as I am,
To tell this story, that you might excuse
His broken promise, and to give this napkin
Dyed in his blood unto the shepherd youth
That he in sport doth call his Rosalind.

ROSALIND swoons

CELIA

Why, how now, Ganymede! sweet Ganymede!

OLIVER

Many will swoon when they do look on blood.

CELIA

There is more in it. Cousin Ganymede!

OLIVER

Look, he recovers.

ROSALIND

I would I were at home.

CELIA

We'll lead you thither.

I pray you, will you take him by the arm?

OLIVER

Be of good cheer, youth. You a man!
You lack a man's heart.

ROSALIND

I do so, I confess it. Ah, sirrah, a body would think this was well counterfeited! I pray you, tell your brother how well I counterfeited. Heigh-ho!

OLIVER

This was not counterfeit; there is too great testimony in your complexion that it was a passion of earnest.

ROSALIND

Counterfeit, I assure you.

OLIVER

Well then, take a good heart and counterfeit to be a man.

ROSALIND

So I do; but, i' faith, I should have been a woman by right.

CELIA

Come, you look paler and paler; pray you, draw homewards. Good sir, go with us.

OLIVER

That will I, for I must bear answer back
How you excuse my brother, Rosalind.

ROSALIND

I shall devise something; but, I pray you, commend my counterfeiting to him. Will you go?

Exeunt

Act 5

SCENE I. THE FOREST.

Enter TOUCHSTONE and AUDREY

TOUCHSTONE

We shall find a time, Audrey; patience, gentle
Audrey.

AUDREY

Faith, the priest was good enough, for all the
old gentleman's saying.

TOUCHSTONE

A most wicked Sir Oliver, Audrey, a most vile
Martext. But, Audrey, there is a youth here in
the forest lays claim to you.

AUDREY

Ay, I know who 'tis; he hath no interest in me
in the world; here comes the man you mean.

TOUCHSTONE

It is meat and drink to me to see a clown. By my troth, we that have good wits have much to answer for; we shall be flouting; we cannot hold.

Enter WILLIAM

WILLIAM

Good even, Audrey.

AUDREY

God ye good even, William.

WILLIAM

And good even to you, sir.

TOUCHSTONE

Good even, gentle friend. Cover thy head, cover thy head; nay, prithee, be covered. How old are you, friend?

WILLIAM

Five and twenty, sir.

TOUCHSTONE

A ripe age. Is thy name William?

WILLIAM

William, sir.

TOUCHSTONE

A fair name. Wast born i' the forest here?

WILLIAM

Ay, sir, I thank God.

TOUCHSTONE

'Thank God;' a good answer. Art rich?

WILLIAM

Faith, sir, so so.

TOUCHSTONE

'So so' is good, very good, very excellent good; and yet it is not; it is but so so. Art thou wise?

WILLIAM

Ay, sir, I have a pretty wit.

TOUCHSTONE

Why, thou sayest well. I do now remember a saying, 'The fool doth think he is wise, but the wise man knows himself to be a fool.' The heathen philosopher, when he had a desire to eat a grape, would open his lips when he put it into his mouth; meaning thereby that grapes were made to eat and lips to open. You do love this maid?

WILLIAM

I do, sir.

TOUCHSTONE

Give me your hand. Art thou learned?

WILLIAM

No, sir.

TOUCHSTONE

Then learn this of me: to have, is to have; for it is a figure in rhetoric that drink, being poured out of a cup into a glass, by filling the one doth empty the other; for all your writers do consent that ipse is he; now, you are not ipse, for I am he.

WILLIAM

Which he, sir?

TOUCHSTONE

He, sir, that must marry this woman. Therefore, you clown, abandon—which is in the vulgar leave—the society—which in the boorish is company—of this female—which in the common is woman—which together is: abandon the society of this female; or, clown, thou perishest; or, to thy better understanding, diest; or, to wit I kill thee, make thee away, translate thy life into death, thy liberty into bondage. I will deal in poison with thee, or in bastinado, or in steel; I will bandy with thee in faction; I will o'errun thee with policy; I will kill thee a hundred and fifty ways; therefore tremble and depart.

AUDREY

Do, good William.

WILLIAM

God rest you merry, sir.

Exit

Enter CORIN

CORIN

Our master and mistress seeks you; come, away, away!

TOUCHSTONE

Trip, Audrey! trip, Audrey! I attend, I attend.

Exeunt

SCENE II. THE FOREST.

Enter ORLANDO and OLIVER

ORLANDO

Is't possible that on so little acquaintance you should like her? that but seeing you should love her? and loving woo? and, wooing, she should grant? and will you persever to enjoy her?

OLIVER

Neither call the giddiness of it in question, the poverty of her, the small acquaintance, my sudden wooing, nor her sudden consenting; but say with me, I love Aliena; say with her that she loves me; consent with both that we may enjoy each other. It shall be to your good; for my father's house and all the revenue that was old Sir Rowland's will I estate upon you, and here live and die a shepherd.

ORLANDO

You have my consent. Let your wedding be to-morrow. Thither will I invite the Duke and all's contented followers. Go you and prepare Aliena; for look you, here comes my Rosalind.

Enter ROSALIND

ROSALIND

God save you, brother.

OLIVER

And you, fair sister.

Exit

ROSALIND

O, my dear Orlando, how it grieves me to see thee wear thy heart in a scarf!

ORLANDO

It is my arm.

ROSALIND

I thought thy heart had been wounded with the claws of a lion.

ORLANDO

Wounded it is, but with the eyes of a lady.

ROSALIND

Did your brother tell you how I counterfeited to swoon when he showed me your handkerchief?

ORLANDO

Ay, and greater wonders than that.

ROSALIND

O, I know where you are. Nay, 'tis true. There
was never any thing so sudden but the fight
of two rams and Caesar's thrasonical brag of
'I came, saw, and overcame.' For your brother
and my sister no sooner met but they looked,
no sooner looked but they loved, no sooner
loved but they sighed, no sooner sighed but
they asked one another the reason, no sooner
knew the reason but they sought the remedy;
and in these degrees have they made a pair
of stairs to marriage which they will climb
incontinent, or else be incontinent before
marriage. They are in the very wrath of love
and they will together; clubs cannot part them.

ORLANDO

They shall be married to-morrow, and I will
bid the Duke to the nuptial. But, O, how bitter
a thing it is to look into happiness through
another man's eyes! By so much the more shall I
to-morrow be at the height of heart-heaviness,
by how much I shall think my brother happy in
having what he wishes for.

ROSALIND

Why then, to-morrow I cannot serve your turn
for Rosalind?

ORLANDO

I can live no longer by thinking.

ROSALIND

I will weary you then no longer with idle talking. Know of me then, for now I speak to some purpose, that I know you are a gentleman of good conceit. I speak not this that you should bear a good opinion of my knowledge, insomuch I say I know you are; neither do I labour for a greater esteem than may in some little measure draw a belief from you, to do yourself good and not to grace me. Believe then, if you please, that I can do strange things. I have, since I was three year old, conversed with a magician, most profound in his art and yet not damnable. If you do love Rosalind so near the heart as your gesture cries it out, when your brother marries Aliena, shall you marry her. I know into what straits of fortune she is driven; and it is not impossible to me, if it appear not inconvenient to you, to set her before your eyes to-morrow human as she is and without any danger.

ORLANDO

Speakest thou in sober meanings?

ROSALIND

By my life, I do; which I tender dearly, though I say I am a magician. Therefore, put you in your best array, bid your friends; for if you will be married to-morrow, you shall, and to Rosalind, if you will.

Enter SILVIUS and PHEBE

Look, here comes a lover of mine and a lover of hers.

PHEBE

Youth, you have done me much ungentleness,
To show the letter that I writ to you.

ROSALIND

I care not if I have. It is my study
To seem despiteful and ungentle to you.
You are there followed by a faithful shepherd;
Look upon him, love him; he worships you.

PHEBE

Good shepherd, tell this youth what 'tis to love.

SILVIUS

It is to be all made of sighs and tears;
And so am I for Phebe.

PHEBE

And I for Ganymede.

ORLANDO

And I for Rosalind.

ROSALIND

And I for no woman.

SILVIUS

It is to be all made of faith and service;
And so am I for Phebe.

PHEBE

And I for Ganymede.

ORLANDO

And I for Rosalind.

ROSALIND

And I for no woman.

SILVIUS

It is to be all made of fantasy,
All made of passion and all made of wishes,
All adoration, duty, and observance,
All humbleness, all patience and impatience,
All purity, all trial, all observance;
And so am I for Phebe.

PHEBE

And so am I for Ganymede.

ORLANDO

And so am I for Rosalind.

ROSALIND

And so am I for no woman.

PHEBE

If this be so, why blame you me to love you?

SILVIUS

If this be so, why blame you me to love you?

ORLANDO

If this be so, why blame you me to love you?

ROSALIND

Who do you speak to, 'Why blame you me to love you?'

ORLANDO

To her that is not here, nor doth not hear.

ROSALIND

Pray you, no more of this; 'tis like the howling of Irish wolves against the moon.

[*To SILVIUS*]

I will help you, if I can.

[*To PHEBE*]

I would love you, if I could. To-morrow meet me all together.

[*To PHEBE*]

I will marry you, if ever I marry woman, and I'll be married to-morrow.

[*To ORLANDO*]

I will satisfy you, if ever I satisfied man, and you shall be married to-morrow.

[*To SILVIUS*]

I will content you, if what pleases you contents you, and you shall be married to-morrow.

[*To ORLANDO*]

As you love Rosalind, meet.

[*To SILVIUS*]

As you love Phebe, meet; and as I love no woman, I'll meet. So fare you well; I have left you commands.

SILVIUS

I'll not fail, if I live.

PHEBE

Nor I.

ORLANDO

Nor I.

Exeunt

SCENE III. THE FOREST.

Enter TOUCHSTONE and AUDREY

TOUCHSTONE

To-morrow is the joyful day, Audrey; to-morrow will we be married.

AUDREY

I do desire it with all my heart; and I hope it is no dishonest desire to desire to be a woman of the world. Here comes two of the banished Duke's pages.

Enter two Pages

FIRST PAGE

Well met, honest gentleman.

TOUCHSTONE

By my troth, well met. Come, sit, sit, and a song.

SECOND PAGE

We are for you; sit i' the middle.

FIRST PAGE

Shall we clap into't roundly, without hawking or spitting or saying we are hoarse, which are the only prologues to a bad voice?

SECOND PAGE

I'faith, i'faith; and both in a tune, like two gipsies on a horse.

SONG

It was a lover and his lass,
     With a hey, and a ho, and a hey nonino,
That o'er the green corn-field did pass
     In the spring time, the only pretty ring time,
When birds do sing, hey ding a ding, ding.
Sweet lovers love the spring.

Between the acres of the rye,
     With a hey, and a ho, and a hey nonino
These pretty country folks would lie,
     In spring time, etc.

This carol they began that hour,
  With a hey, and a ho, and a hey nonino,
How that a life was but a flower
  In spring time, etc.

And therefore take the present time,
  With a hey, and a ho, and a hey nonino;
For love is crowned with the prime
  In spring time, etc.

TOUCHSTONE

Truly, young gentlemen, though there was no great matter in the ditty, yet the note was very untuneable.

FIRST PAGE

You are deceived, sir; we kept time, we lost not our time.

TOUCHSTONE

By my troth, yes; I count it but time lost to hear such a foolish song. God be wi' you; and God mend your voices! Come, Audrey.

Exeunt

SCENE IV. THE FOREST.

Enter DUKE SENIOR, AMIENS, JAQUES, ORLANDO, OLIVER, and CELIA

DUKE SENIOR

    Dost thou believe, Orlando, that the boy

    Can do all this that he hath promised?

ORLANDO

    I sometimes do believe, and sometimes do not;

    As those that fear they hope, and know they
        fear.

    Enter ROSALIND, SILVIUS, and PHEBE

ROSALIND

    Patience once more, whiles our compact is
        urged:

    You say, if I bring in your Rosalind,

    You will bestow her on Orlando here?

DUKE SENIOR

    That would I, had I kingdoms to give with her.

ROSALIND

    And you say, you will have her, when I bring
        her?

ORLANDO

    That would I, were I of all kingdoms king.

ROSALIND

    You say, you'll marry me, if I be willing?

PHEBE

That will I, should I die the hour after.

ROSALIND

But if you do refuse to marry me,

You'll give yourself to this most faithful shepherd?

PHEBE

So is the bargain.

ROSALIND

You say, that you'll have Phebe, if she will?

SILVIUS

Though to have her and death were both one thing.

ROSALIND

I have promised to make all this matter even.

Keep you your word, O Duke, to give your daughter;

You yours, Orlando, to receive his daughter;

Keep your word, Phebe, that you'll marry me,

Or else refusing me, to wed this shepherd;

Keep your word, Silvius, that you'll marry her.

If she refuse me; and from hence I go,

To make these doubts all even.

Exeunt ROSALIND
and CELIA

DUKE SENIOR

    I do remember in this shepherd boy

    Some lively touches of my daughter's favour.

ORLANDO

    My lord, the first time that I ever saw him

    Methought he was a brother to your daughter.

    But, my good lord, this boy is forest-born,

    And hath been tutor'd in the rudiments

    Of many desperate studies by his uncle,

    Whom he reports to be a great magician,

    Obscured in the circle of this forest.

    Enter TOUCHSTONE and AUDREY

JAQUES

    There is, sure, another flood toward, and these couples are coming to the ark. Here comes a pair of very strange beasts, which in all tongues are called fools.

TOUCHSTONE

    Salutation and greeting to you all!

JAQUES

    Good my lord, bid him welcome. This is the motley-minded gentleman that I have so often met in the forest. He hath been a courtier, he swears.

TOUCHSTONE

    If any man doubt that, let him put me to my purgation. I have trod a measure; I have flattered a lady; I have been politic with my friend, smooth with mine enemy; I have undone three tailors; I have had four quarrels, and like to have fought one.

JAQUES

And how was that ta'en up?

TOUCHSTONE

Faith, we met, and found the quarrel was upon the seventh cause.

JAQUES

How seventh cause? Good my lord, like this fellow.

DUKE SENIOR

I like him very well.

TOUCHSTONE

God 'ild you, sir; I desire you of the like. I press in here, sir, amongst the rest of the country copulatives, to swear and to forswear, according as marriage binds and blood breaks. A poor virgin, sir, an ill-favoured thing, sir, but mine own; a poor humour of mine, sir, to take that that no man else will. Rich honesty dwells like a miser, sir, in a poor house; as your pearl in your foul oyster.

DUKE SENIOR

By my faith, he is very swift and sententious.

TOUCHSTONE

According to the fool's bolt, sir, and such dulcet diseases.

JAQUES

But, for the seventh cause; how did you find the quarrel on the seventh cause?

TOUCHSTONE

Upon a lie seven times removed—bear your body more seeming, Audrey—as thus, sir. I did dislike the cut of a certain courtier's beard; he sent me word, if I said his beard was not cut well, he was in the mind it was. This is called the Retort Courteous. If I sent him word again 'it was not well cut,' he would send me word, he cut it to please himself. This is called the Quip Modest. If again 'it was not well cut,' he disabled my judgment. This is called the Reply Churlish. If again 'it was not well cut,' he would answer, I spake not true. This is called the Reproof Valiant. If again 'it was not well cut,' he would say I lied. This is called the Countercheque Quarrelsome. And so to the Lie Circumstantial and the Lie Direct.

JAQUES

And how oft did you say his beard was not well cut?

TOUCHSTONE

I durst go no further than the Lie Circumstantial, nor he durst not give me the Lie Direct; and so we measured swords and parted.

JAQUES

Can you nominate in order now the degrees of the lie?

TOUCHSTONE

O sir, we quarrel in print, by the book; as you have books for good manners. I will name you the degrees. The first, the Retort Courteous; the second, the Quip Modest; the third, the Reply Churlish; the fourth, the Reproof Valiant; the fifth, the Countercheque Quarrelsome; the sixth, the Lie with Circumstance; the seventh, the Lie Direct. All these you may avoid but the Lie Direct; and you may avoid that too, with an If. I knew when seven justices could not take up a quarrel, but when the parties were met themselves, one of them thought but of an If, as, 'If you said so, then I said so;' and they shook hands and swore brothers. Your If is the only peacemaker; much virtue in If.

JAQUES

Is not this a rare fellow, my lord? He's as good at any thing and yet a fool.

DUKE SENIOR

> He uses his folly like a stalking horse and under
> the presentation of that he shoots his wit.
>
> *Enter HYMEN,*
> *ROSALIND, and CELIA*
> *Still Music*

HYMEN

> Then is there mirth in heaven,
> When earthly things made even
> Atone together.
> Good Duke, receive thy daughter
> Hymen from heaven brought her,
> Yea, brought her hither,
> That thou mightst join her hand with his
> Whose heart within his bosom is.

ROSALIND

> [*To DUKE SENIOR*] To you I give myself, for
>   I am yours.
> [*To ORLANDO*]
> To you I give myself, for I am yours.

DUKE SENIOR

> If there be truth in sight, you are my daughter.

ORLANDO

> If there be truth in sight, you are my Rosalind.

PHEBE

> If sight and shape be true,
> Why then, my love adieu!

ROSALIND

I'll have no father, if you be not he;

I'll have no husband, if you be not he;

Nor ne'er wed woman, if you be not she.

HYMEN

Peace, ho! I bar confusion;

'Tis I must make conclusion

Of these most strange events.

Here's eight that must take hands

To join in Hymen's bands,

If truth holds true contents.

You and you no cross shall part;

You and you are heart in heart

You to his love must accord,

Or have a woman to your lord;

You and you are sure together,

As the winter to foul weather.

Whiles a wedlock-hymn we sing,

Feed yourselves with questioning;

That reason wonder may diminish,

How thus we met, and these things finish.

SONG

Wedding is great Juno's crown;

O blessed bond of board and bed!

'Tis Hymen peoples every town;

High wedlock then be honoured.

Honour, high honour and renown,
To Hymen, god of every town!
DUKE SENIOR

O my dear niece, welcome thou art to me!
Even daughter, welcome, in no less degree.
PHEBE

I will not eat my word, now thou art mine;
Thy faith my fancy to thee doth combine.
Enter JAQUES DE BOYS
JAQUES DE BOYS

Let me have audience for a word or two.
I am the second son of old Sir Rowland,
That bring these tidings to this fair assembly.
Duke Frederick, hearing how that every day
Men of great worth resorted to this forest,
Address'd a mighty power; which were on foot,
In his own conduct, purposely to take
His brother here and put him to the sword;
And to the skirts of this wild wood he came;
Where meeting with an old religious man,
After some question with him, was converted
Both from his enterprise and from the world,
His crown bequeathing to his banish'd brother,
And all their lands restored to them again
That were with him exiled. This to be true,
I do engage my life.

DUKE SENIOR

> Welcome, young man;
> Thou offer'st fairly to thy brothers' wedding:
> To one his lands withheld, and to the other
> A land itself at large, a potent dukedom.
> First, in this forest, let us do those ends
> That here were well begun and well begot;
> And after, every of this happy number
> That have endured shrewd days and nights
>   with us
> Shall share the good of our returned fortune,
> According to the measure of their states.
> Meantime, forget this new-fall'n dignity
> And fall into our rustic revelry.
> Play, music! And you, brides and bridegrooms
>   all,
> With measure heap'd in joy, to the measures
>   fall.

JAQUES

> Sir, by your patience. If I heard you rightly,
> The Duke hath put on a religious life
> And thrown into neglect the pompous court?

JAQUES DE BOYS

> He hath.

JAQUES

> To him will I. Out of these convertites
> There is much matter to be heard and learn'd.

[*To DUKE SENIOR*]
You to your former honour I bequeath;
Your patience and your virtue well deserves it.
[*To ORLANDO*]
You to a love that your true faith doth merit;
[*To OLIVER*]
You to your land and love and great allies;
[*To SILVIUS*]
You to a long and well-deserved bed;
[*To TOUCHSTONE*]
And you to wrangling; for thy loving voyage
Is but for two months victuall'd. So, to your
    pleasures;
I am for other than for dancing measures.

DUKE SENIOR
    Stay, Jaques, stay.

JAQUES
    To see no pastime I what you would have
    I'll stay to know at your abandon'd cave.

                                        Exit

DUKE SENIOR
    Proceed, proceed. We will begin these rites,
    As we do trust they'll end, in true delights.
                A dance

                                        Exeunt

EPILOGUE

ROSALIND

It is not the fashion to see the lady the epilogue; but it is no more unhandsome than to see the lord the prologue. If it be true that good wine needs no bush, 'tis true that a good play needs no epilogue; yet to good wine they do use good bushes, and good plays prove the better by the help of good epilogues. What a case am I in then, that am neither a good epilogue nor cannot insinuate with you in the behalf of a good play! I am not furnished like a beggar, therefore to beg will not become me. My way is to conjure you; and I'll begin with the women. I charge you, O women, for the love you bear to men, to like as much of this play as please you; and I charge you, O men, for the love you bear to women—as I perceive by your simpering, none of you hates them—that between you and the women the play may please. If I were a woman I would kiss as many of you as had beards that pleased me, complexions that liked me and breaths that I defied not; and, I am sure, as many as have good beards or good faces or sweet breaths will, for my kind offer, when I make curtsy, bid me farewell.

Exeunt